GENESIS

THE BOOK OF BEGINNINGS

— A DEVOTIONAL COMMENTARY —

DR. DONALD O. PHILLIPS

GENESIS

THE BOOK OF BEGINNINGS

— A DEVOTIONAL COMMENTARY —

DR. DONALD O. PHILLIPS

All Scriptures are taken from the King James Bible.

ISBN# 978-1-935075-77-6

Printed in the United States of America.

Printed by Calvary Publishing
A Ministry of Parker Memorial Baptist Church
1902 East Cavanaugh Road
Lansing, Michigan 48910
www.CalvaryPublishing.org

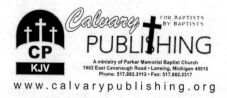

Calvary PUBLISHING
FOR BAPTISTS
BY BAPTISTS
CP KJV
A ministry of Parker Memorial Baptist Church
1902 East Cavanaugh Road • Lansing, Michigan 48910
Phone: 517.882.2112 • Fax: 517.882.2317
www.calvarypublishing.org

Dedication

This book is dedicated to Mom and Dad who took me to the House of God. Thanks.

Acknowledgements

Thanks to Donna Phillips and Calvary Publishing for their help with this book.

Contents

Author's Preface

The book of Genesis is the most unique book in Scripture. The Doctrines of Scripture are found in germ in Genesis. Creation unfolds before us, and earth is the scene of Bible History. Jesus Christ is revealed to us in this first book of the Bible.

INTRODUCTION

Genesis means origin, source, birth or beginning. In the Book of Beginnings we have the beginning of everything but God. Authorship belongs to
Moses. The Old Testament and the New Testament
shows Moses to be the Author of the Pentateuch.
Joshua 1:7; Daniel 9:11-13; Luke 16:29; John 7:19;
Acts 26:22; and Romans 10:19. In Genesis we see
the beginning of the material universe. Human race,
Human sin, Prophecy of Redemption, Human family life, Godless civilization, Nations, confusion of
Language, Hebrew Race, The Fall of Lucifer and
much more. Genesis is the Book of first mention,
and has been called the seed plot of the Bible. It is
germform for almost all great doctrines afterward
developed.

The Key Word is "Beginning." The Message –
"The failure of Man under every condition met by
the Salvation of God." There are two books in the
Bible that Satan especially hates, and tries to dis-
credit, Genesis and Revelation. Why does he hate
them? They both prophesy his downfall. Genesis
tells us who would bring it about, and Revelation
gives the details of his judgment. Again Genesis
is perhaps the most important book in the Bible.
Genesis is the seed plot of the whole Bible. It is the

foundation on which Divine Revelation rests and on which it is built up.

There are four main events in Genesis:
1. Creation 1:1
2. Fall 3:1
3. Flood 6:1
4. Nations 10:1

There are four main people:
1. Abraham 12:1
2. Isaac 25:19
3. Jacob 27:19
4. Joseph 37:1 – 50:26

Genesis opens in a garden and closes in a coffin. The first eleven chapters cover over 2000 years in telling of the origin of the universe and the race of man. From Genesis 12 on thru the rest of the Old Testament is 2000 years, dealing with Abraham and his family. Creation to Abraham 2000 years, Abraham to Jesus 2000 years.

There were six literal days of creation. God created the world and all that is in it in six days. Then he declared it all to be very good, 1:31. The Creator rested on the seventh day 2:1-3. He rested not because He was tired, but because He was done with Creation. The gap theory says that Creation 1:1, was followed by catastrophe 1:2, and then was succeeded by Gods re-creation of the physical world. I do not believe it was a re-creation, but Creation.

Man and Woman are the crowning achievements of Gods creative work. Genesis shows that God first came down to create then to do a work of redemption. To create He had only to speak. To redeem His fallen creature, He had to suffer. He made man by His own breath; He saves him by His own Blood. Genesis introduces us typically to Gods purpose and plan in redemption, 3:15, 21; 22:8. Galatians 4:4, 5; John 1:29; Matthew 20:28.

In Genesis we have in verse one the commencement of time, and we find the scene of Bible History, "the earth."

Chapter 1

Verse 1

The Holy Spirit at once introduces us to God. The purpose in creation is to have a sphere in which He might display His eternal power and Godhead. God reveals Himself. He makes Himself known by His works. "In the beginning…" God created, not formed from any preexisting materials, but made out of nothing, "…the heaven and the earth." The whole universe was produced by the creative power of God. Acts17:24 and Romans 11:36. It is amazing, and yet you find that the creation story is a very brief story, read Genesis 1:1 again, ten words.

There was no earth, but God made an earth, there was no water, but God made the water. God made everything out of nothing. Hebrews 11:3. Hebrews 11 is important because the believing heart will believe that God created the heavens and the earth. Creation is a spiritual truth that must be received by faith. There are no witnesses to the creation but God Himself. It is through faith that we understand that the worlds were framed by the Word of God. Hebrews 11:3.

Read verse two. The earth itself was brought forth "…without form and void…" that is, the material, the matter of the earth itself was created. Like the potter and the clay. The potter at first had a lump of clay from which something beautiful would be formed.

Verse 2

The Spirit of God begins to work, and wonderful things God had in mind. What joy God had in making all things in which when He seen it, said "_...
it was_ very good."

Verse 3

Does this mean that there was light before there was any sun? Yes. The sun was not created until the fourth day. It is not true that all light and energy comes from the sun. Genesis 1:3, 4, shows that God created light. All light is really from God. God may use the sun for a time to dispense light, but He is not bound to any limitations. Read Revelation 21:23, 24. The earth was created before the sun. The sun was made to serve the earth, because the earth was made for man. The earth was the place where redemption would be wrought. The words of verse three are Gods first words recorded in Scripture. "And God said..."

Verses 1-5

Constitute the first day of creation.

Verses 6-8

Constitute the Second Day of Creation. We have here the separation of upper and lower waters. On the first day the earth was still of dominantly watery aspect. We have on the Second day a separation. The power required for such a tremendous separation comes from God's spoken Word: Let there be a firmament in the midst of the waters. The lower waters would provide a protective canopy for earths in habitants, and the space between would provide an atmospheric reservoir to maintain the breath of life.

The word "firmament" in Hebrew means "expanse" which is synonymous with our modern word, "space." There are three heavens:

1. Birds fly – Jeremiah 4:25
2. Stars - Isaiah 13:10
3. Gods Throne – Hebrews 9:24

On the earth the lower waters would be gathered into the seas. The upper waters would be water vapor. Water canopy. The earth before the flood was sub tropical climate, which dissipated after the flood.

Verses 9-13

Constitute the Third day. The waters under the firmament were a shore less ocean. On the third day of creation, a third act of division was accomplished by God. The light had been divided from the darkness on the first day; the waters above the firmament divided from the waters below the firmament on the second day, and now the dry land from the lower waters on the third day. When dry land appeared on earth there is a lot to consider, not only had rocks and minerals been formed, but also so had a blanket of fertile soil, sand, silt, clay with all the chemical nutrients needed. God spoke and all that was needed was there. Three main orders of plant life are mentioned: <u>Grass</u> – including all spreading ground covering vegetation. <u>Herbs</u> – including all bushes and shrubs. <u>Trees</u> – includes all large woody plants, including fruit bearing trees.

These plants were made not as seeds but, as full-grown plants, whose seed was in themselves. Adam was created as full-grown man, the trees were created as full-grown trees, and the whole universe was made as a functioning entity, complete and fully developed.

Verse 11

"<u>...after his kind...</u>" – This blows the evolutionist who talks about "<u>new kinds.</u>" There can be "horizontal variation," but, no "vertical" changes. No changes from Creation. What God created produced after its kind, because its seed was in itself. Notice further, <u>I Corinthians 15:38, 39</u>.

Verses 14-19

Constitute the Fourth Day. On the first day God said "<u>Let there be light...</u>" On the fourth day God said, "<u>Let there be lights...</u>" or light givers. Verse fourteen – God keeps a calendar. Time is the managed, controlled servant of God. God used a day for a unit of time. He starts with a day, and then puts His clock in the sky so men can keep account of the days by the revolution of the earth around the sun. The sun rules the day, the moon the night. There was light on the first day God directed the light. The Sun could fit six million moons inside it. Many worship the Sun, Moon, and Stars. The Star Antares could swallow up to 64 million suns. God used five words to tell us of the stars of space. <u>1:16</u> – "<u>...he made the stars also.</u>" God uses 50 chapters about the construction and significance of the Tabernacle. Think of it 50 chapters about the Tabernacle, five words about the stars. God looks at things differently than man. The Bible is a handbook of redemption. You see creation was nothing for God, He had only to speak. But to redeem, He had to suffer. It is said by Sir James Jeans that there are more stars in space than there are grains of sand on all the seashores of all the world. God is more interested in people than He is in planets, more interested in souls than in stars.

Verses 20-23

Constitute the Fifth Day. By the time that we arrive on the fifth day all necessities for living creatures were present on the earth, light, air, water, soil, chemicals, plants, fruits and so on. Before the fifth day the earth was void of inhabitants. God formed it to be inhabited. Isaiah 45:18.

Verse 20

"And God said, Let the waters bring forth abundantly..." What this means is the waters suddenly at Gods Word swarmed abundantly with creatures.

Verse 21

"...that hath life..." – The word "life" occurs for the first time here.

Verse 22

Not only did God pronounce in Verse 21 "...and God saw that *it was* good." but He also pronounced a blessing upon the animals. The blessing included both a command and a provision for the continued multiplication of the animals. God gave a similar command to the animals after the flood. Genesis 8:17.

Verses 24-31

Constitute the Sixth Day. Now animals must be formed for the land surfaces.

Verse 24

"...Let the earth bring forth the living creature..." That is their bodies were composed of the elements

of the earth, and when they died they would go back
to the earth.

"Cattle" – Here we have domestic animals.

"Creeping thing" – Animals that crawl or creep
close to the surface of the ground.

"Beasts" – Wild animals.

Verse 26

The creation of man is the last and highest of life.
Every step in creation so far is preparation for man.
This world was purposed for a higher being than fish,
foul or beast. What uses have animals for coal, iron,
copper, oil, gas, gold, silver, pearls and diamonds?
They have no capacity to enjoy the beauty of the
landscape. They cannot measure the distances to
the stars. They cannot worship and adore God.

This is a contrast between the language of the
creation of man and animals, for the first time in
Verse 26, "Let us make man in our image." Man
is not a higher order of an animal, man is created
in the image of God. Man is a rational, moral, and
spiritual being. This image of God involves much.
Knowledge and reason, Colossians 3:10;

Genesis 2:19-20. Uprightness and holiness,
Ecclesiastes 7:29; Ephesians 4:24. The will, we are
a free moral agent. Worship and Communion with
God. There is an uncrossable gulf made between
man and beast. Man can make and play musical

instruments, and write songs. Man has moral consciousness, not like animals.

CHAPTER 2

Verses 1-3

When God finished His six days of work, He looked upon it and it was very good. Verses 1 thru 3 are a summary that God had now completed His work of creation. His work of creation was finished and He rested because He was done, but He did not rest long. Remember 1000 years, like a day to God. <u>Psalms 90:4; II Peter 3:8</u>. He soon had the work of redemption. Man sinned, God went to work again. When the Son of God on the cross shouted the mighty cry of victory. <u>"It is finished."</u> Then once again God rested on the Sabbath day, in Joseph's tomb until the dawning of the first day of the new week. When we receive Christ as Saviour we enter into <u>rest</u>.

We find something now in chapter 2 that is the law of recurrence. In chapter 1 we have the account of creation in chapter 2 God is going over the events of the six days of creation. In this second chapter God describes in greater detail certain events of the sixth day.

Verses 4-6

We now see the purpose of God in chapter 1. In chapter 1 God was preparing a home for the man whom He made. God is now getting ready to move this man into the place that He has prepared for him.

We have organic life, then animal life, and then Gods crowning creation, <u>Man</u>.

Verse 7

Physically man was taken out of the ground. Our bodies are made up of about 15 or 16 chemical elements. Those same chemical elements are in the ground. If we were to be boiled down into the separate chemical elements of which we were made we would be worth a couple of bucks. That is the extent of our bodily worth because we were made out of the dust of the ground. Yet man is more than dust <u>Psalms 139:14</u>, the glory is all the Lord's, we have nothing to boast about.

"<u>...and breathed into his nostrils the breath of life...</u>" The dust was dust until God touched it and put life into it. God gave man life physical and spiritual. Man has a capacity for God. Man's body has been completely formed, equipped with nostrils, lungs, bones, organs etc, but was lifeless. It must be energized. The breathing mechanism must be activated, the heart must start to pump and circulate the blood. Life can only come from life, and the living God is the only self-existent Being, and so life comes from Him. The breath of life is shared by animals, but they at a distance, only to man did God directly "breath into his nostrils the breath of life."

"...and man became a living soul." The soul of man is not of the earth as is the body. I Corinthians 15:45, 47. The soul is the man, "you are a soul." The spirit is that part of man which knows the intellect or mind. I Corinthians 2:4. The soul is the seat of the will, appetite, affection, and desire.

Verse 8

Bible History can be summarized with four gardens:

1. Eden, where sin entered
2. Gethsemane, where Christ yielded to death
3. Calvary, where He died and was buried and rose again
4. Heavenly Paradise, Man was created outside the Garden and placed in it, while the woman was created in the garden

Verse 9

God placed Adam in the garden and made everything good, for Adam's enjoyment. There were two trees that were different. The Tree of Life was in the midst of the garden. This tree was a sign and seal to Adam assuring him of continuance of life and happiness. Then there is the, "tree of knowledge of good and evil." This tree symbolized the authority of God. To eat of this tree meant to disobey God, and receive the penalty of death.

Verse 10-14

This river contributed much to the pleasantness and the fruitfulness of the garden. <u>Revelation 22:1</u>.

Verse 15

Paradise itself was not exempt from work. None of us was sent into the world to be idle. There is pleasure in the business, which God calls us to. While Adam was about his work, his heart was with God.

Verse 16

Here we see Gods graciousness. An allowance of liberty and an assurance of life to Adam and immortal life upon his obedience.

Verse 17

Adam was a perfect creature, having never sinned, but he had the ability to sin. It was necessary for Adam to be tempted. God wants His creatures to love and obey Him of their own free will, and not because they have too. To be a free moral agent, must have the power to choose. Adam and Eve enjoyed liberty and abundant provision in the Garden and did not need the fruit from the tree of knowledge of good and evil.

"...<u>thou shalt surely die</u>." The death of the body is the separation of soul and spirit from the body. The death of soul and spirit is their separation from God. This is the death that Adam died, and in Adam

we died also. The death we died in Adam is overcome only by the vicarious death of the Lord Jesus
Christ. By passing through Adam's death, we received death. By passing through Christ's death we
receive life. Adam should have obeyed God merely
as an expression of his love.

Verse 18

Everything in creation was "<u>very good</u>," except
the loneliness of Adam. "<u>...*It is* not good that the
man should be alone...</u>" this is the basis for marriage:

1. Companionship
2. To carry on the race
3. To help one another

The true idea of the woman is that she should be
man's compliment, to fill up that which is lacking in
him.

God created the home as the perfect triangle,
the man, the woman, and the Lord. <u>Ecclesiastes
4:12</u>. As long as the Lord has His proper place in
the home it is sure.

Verse 19

It is not likely that all these animals actually lived
in the Garden of Eden. God must have directed them
to come to Adam. As the animals passed in review,
Adam gave each a quick appraisal and an appropri-

ate name was given. We see Adam's high intelligence and quick discernment. <u>No cave man</u>.

Verse 20

As one after another of the animals passed before Adam no doubt in pairs male and female. Adam could not help but be impressed with his own uniqueness, for all the animals there was a mate, but for Adam there was not found an helpmate for him. God never awakens a desire that He cannot and will not satisfy.

Verse 21

We have here the first surgical operation. God made the first woman from man instead of from the ground like He did with man.

Verse 22-25

First marriage. Marriage is honorable, <u>Hebrews 13:4.</u> This was quite a marriage, for God Himself gave the bride away. He made them one. God Himself puts His authority where society and government pronounce a marriage. A legal marriage accepted on earth and in Heaven. Bound by the laws of God and man.

Marriage – One man, one woman, one lifetime. Polygamy, divorce, adultery, promiscuity, and other distortions of the marriage covenant have permeated many cultures.

Verse 24

Man is responsible to his wife and is no longer under the control of his father and mother. Man is to make his wife happy. The wife is to take care of her husband.

Verse 25

They were innocent with no consciousness of sin or moral guilt. God commanded them to "... Be fruitful, and multiply..." There was no sin, and no shame.

CHAPTER 3

Verse 1

Before man could bring sin into the world, he must be persuaded to sin by an agent external to himself, since there was as yet nothing within his own nature to lead him in such direction. The serpent was a colorful, bright and beautiful animal whose movements were smooth and graceful. The serpent was more clever than any of the other animals. In her innocence, the woman was dazzled and led astray by this subtle creature. The Bible later identifies that "old serpent" as the devil. Revelation 12:9, 20:2.

First question. It was intended to cast doubt upon the Word of God. God said

but Satan asks if God had really spoken. Here is the first denial of divine revelation and divine inspiration.

The Temptation, Genesis 3:1-6

1. The Tempter – God is not the author of sin, nor does He tempt men to sin, this is the work of the devil. Satan was a beautiful angel originally, but his sin ruined him. Isaiah 14:12-17.

Ezekiel 28:11-19. Satan comes to Eve under the guise of the serpent, he never appears in his true character. Remember: "Temptation is connected with the beautiful, its real character is hidden." In

Genesis 3, Satan is the serpent who deceives, in Genesis 4, he is the lion that murders.

2. The Target – Satan aimed at Eve's mind and succeeded in deceiving her. II Corinthians 11:1-3. We find in scripture that man's mind is part of being created in God's image. Colossians 3:9,10, so Satan attacks God when he attacks the mind. Satan uses lies. John 8:44 – "...for he is liar, and the father of it."

3. The Tactic – As long as the mind holds to God's truth, Satan cannot win, but once the mind doubts God's Word, there is room for the devil's lies. Satan questioned God's Word 3:1, denied God's Word 3:4, and then substituted his own lies, Satan's Doctrine, 3:5. Satan seeks to undermine the goodness of God, he suggests that God is "holding out on them" by keeping them from the tree of knowledge of good and evil. When we question God's goodness and doubt His love, we are playing right into the hand of Satan. Satan makes the temptation sound wonderful by making an offer. "...ye shall be as gods..." Remember Satan wanted to be like the most High. Isaiah 14:14, and centuries later, he offered Christ all the Kingdoms of the world in Matthew 4:8.

4. The Tragedy – Eve should not have "given place to the devil" she should have held to God's Word and resisted him. In Eve's reply to Satan she both added to and subtracted from God's actual words,

leaving an effect of making God <u>seem less generous</u> and <u>more demanding</u> than He really was. Eve took from the Word in <u>3:2</u> by <u>omitting "freely"</u> 2:16. She added to the Word in <u>3:3</u> by adding <u>"touch it."</u> God had not forbidden them to touch the fruit, we see Eve's resentment by this supposed restriction. Eve changed the Word in <u>3:3</u> by making God's, <u>"…thou shalt surely die…"</u> 2:17 into <u>"…lest ye die."</u>

It is always dangerous to alter God's Word, either by <u>addition,</u> (as do <u>modern cultists</u>) or by <u>subtraction</u>. (As do <u>modern liberals</u>).

Notice <u>James 4:7</u>. How do we resist the devil? <u>We resist the devil by maintaining faith in God's Word</u>. <u>Philippians 2:5-8</u>.

Remember Satan says that God's Word is not true <u>3:4</u>. <u>2:17</u> – <u>"…thou shalt surely die."</u> Satan is a liar and he still clings to his lie, today he denies the eternity of the lake of fire. He teaches soul – sleep and soul annihilation. He preaches the second chance of salvation after death.

Further comments on Chapter 3

The other books of the Bible both Old Testament and New Testament are rooted in the 3rd chapter of Genesis. This chapter explains the necessity for redemption, and gives the first promise of redemption. <u>3:15</u>

<u>In chapter three we have the</u>:

1. <u>The Tempter</u>
2. <u>The Tempted</u>
3. <u>The Temptation</u>
4. <u>The woman's sin</u>
5. <u>The man's sin</u>
6. <u>The threefold result</u>
   A. The awakening of conscience
   B. Shame
   C. Hiding

1. <u>The Tempter</u> – <u>was an actual serpent</u>. Paul says the serpent beguiled Eve.

<u>II Corinthians 11:3</u>. Satan is called, the Devil, that old serpent. <u>Revelation 12:9, 20:2</u>. How did he deceive Eve? <u>II Corinthians 11:13 -14</u>. Eve surely did not know she was talking to the devil. There is a miracle here in that the serpent talked. Eve knew that no beast or reptile had ever talked before. She was deceived in that she surely thought that this was from God.

2. <u>The Tempted</u> – <u>Who did the serpent tempt</u>? <u>The woman</u>. <u>I Timothy 2:11 – 15</u>. The woman is the weaker vessel. <u>I Peter 3:7</u>. Satan believed he could get to the man through the woman.

3. <u>The Temptation</u> – <u>3:1</u> – "... And he said unto the woman, Yea, hath God said, Ye shall not eat of every tree of the garden?" Satan is trying to cast doubt upon the Word of God. This temptation Satan could never have brought before Adam because

Adam knew God said it. God spoke directly with Adam. God gave this command to Adam before Eve was made. Eve got the command from Adam. You see why Satan went to Eve? Satan comes to you and me the same way today. Satan would not go to Paul and say, "Did the Lord Jesus Christ give that gospel to you to preach?" But Satan will come to us today and say, "Did the Lord Jesus Christ give that gospel to Paul?" Notice, Luke 16:27-31. And so Satan comes and tries to issue doubt concerning Gods Word. Romans 10:17 – "So then faith *cometh* by hearing, and hearing by the word of God."

4. The woman's sin – Satan calls attention to the only limitation of Gods command, Genesis 2:17 and not to the broad permission of the command. 2:16. Satan says to Eve "In limiting you, this way is God good?" Now if he loved you why did he not say, you can eat the fruit of any of these trees? That is why the Bible says in 3:1 – "Now the serpent was more subtil than any beast of the field…" Satan knew that if Eve would eat of the forbidden fruit that she would die. Man today is deceived when he thinks he can sin and not pay the penalty. Notice – 3:6 – "…she took of the fruit thereof, and did eat, and gave also unto her husband with her; and he did eat." Now who tempted Adam? The woman. Milton's statement of Adam's reason for sinning, to stand by his wife even if she went to hell. Over in France, when some great man who

has been loved, trusted and honored suddenly falls, the first question they ask is, "who is the woman."

5. The man's sin – Nobody pulled the wool over Adam's eyes. He was not deceived. He knew what God said. He never doubted God's Word. He deliberately ate of that fruit because the woman asked him. Adam's sin was greater than Eve's sin. Death came upon all men not because of Eve's sin, but because of Adam's sin. We fell in Adam. Romans 5:12 – 14. Adam simply preferred the woman to God. Remember Solomon? I Kings 11:1 – 13. 6. The three fold results

A. The awakening of conscience 3:5, 7. Conscience - is that inward monitor that passes judgment on the rightfulness of our actions. Before God said a thing to Adam and Eve their conscience pronounced judgment.

B. Shame Verse 7 – Not only did they see their physical nakedness but also their spiritual nakedness.

C. Hiding Verse 8 – Shame then fear followed. Proverbs 28:1

Verse 21

The first bloodshed in the Bible was for sin. Verse 15, 17.

Verse 22

We see here the Trinity, "…the man is become as

one of us…" This likeness was certainly not that of any of God's wonderful attributes. <u>Man now knows the difference between good and evil.</u> Notice what God said long after this time. <u>Jeremiah 4:22</u> – If a man stepped off an airplane wing at 20,000 feet without a parachute, he would be up in the air like the pilot who could say, "That man has become as one of us, to know altitude and gravity." But there would be no power to maintain altitude or to avoid gravity. <u>"lest he put forth his hand, and take also of the tree of life, and eat, and live for ever:"</u> How kind God was to prevent man from laying hold on something that would have kept him forever in his lost condition of death. How terrible it would be to live forever as we are now. What makes life bearable is that we are going to heaven.

Verse 24

Man coming to God, must now be through a blood sacrifice.

CHAPTER 4

Genesis 3
1. Beginning of sin
2. Individual sin
3. Sin against God

Genesis 4
1. Fruit of sin – Murder
2. Family sin
3. Sin against man

Sin cannot be controlled, it has a snowball effect.

Verse 1

First birth. Eve knew of <u>Genesis 3:15</u> and perhaps believed that her child would be the answer and that they would soon be back in Eden. <u>Cain</u> – But the baby turned out to be a murderer. <u>Eve was learning what spiritual death really meant.</u> From this point it would be along time before the Saviour would come, about 4,000 years. Adam and Eve were beginning to see what their sin had done. That is the consequences.

Verse 2

<u>Abel</u> – <u>Vanity.</u> When Eve thought she had obtained the promised seed in Cain, she was so taken up in this that by the time Abel was born <u>he was as vanity to her.</u> <u>Both their occupations were honorable.</u> <u>Cain provided food, Abel provided clothing.</u> It may be that man was not authorized until after the flood to use animals for food. <u>Notice</u> – <u>Genesis</u>

1:29, 2:16, 3:19 9:3.
   "And in process of time…"

Verse 3

   We know from Hebrews 11:4 that Abel's offering
was by "faith," and so he obeying God's command,
there must have been a day of atonement commanded by God. For worship "a day," the Sabbath
was never known until the time of Moses. Nehemiah 9:14. "An offering unto the Lord." We are not to
bring what seems best to us but what He desires. It
is not enough to worship God in our own way, we
must worship in His way. John 4:24 His way always
points to Christ. This is contrary to all cults.

Verse 4

   Abel did not pick a blemished lamb, but the fin-
est. Nothing is too good for God. Here the first lamb
is seen, one lamb for one man. Then in Exodus 12
we have the Passover, one lamb for one household.
Then Leviticus 16 on the Day of Atonement it was
one sacrifice for the nation. Finally it is Christ who
takes away the sin of the world. John 1:29 And so we
progress from one lamb for one man to the Lamb of
God which takes away the sin of the world.

Verse 5

   God had respect unto Abel's offering. Blood but
not unto Cain's. Cain thought his beautiful fruit of-

fering was more suitable than a <u>blood sacrifice</u>. He wished to consider the holiness of beauty rather then the beauty of holiness. Cain would be like a man strolling up Fifth Avenue in an Easter Parade after attending a church service where the Resurrection of Jesus is denied. <u>There are a lot of Cain's today.</u>

"...<u>Cain was very wroth...</u>" The old nature becomes its angriest when it's crossed. Wanting ones own way is the worst of sins because it is the first of sins. It leads to all others, because God and His interest stand as the barrier to self and its interest.

"<u>...his countenance fell.</u>" The mouth speaks out of the abundance of the heart, the face reflects the thoughts of the hearts.

One came his way the other came God's way. <u>Blood divides</u>.

Verse 6

"<u>And the LORD said unto Cain...</u>" We see the marvelous <u>Grace of God here</u> in that He would stoop down and talk with this sinner. <u>Why did not God destroy Cain?</u> Cain was a murderer in his heart before He was with His hands. Instead God pleaded with this sinner as He does with all. "<u>God is Love</u>," even Cain was loved by God. <u>Notice – Matthew 22:12, 26:50.</u> Here Cain was angry with God when he should have been angry with himself, this shows his unhumbled heart.

Verse 7

If you, Cain, will repent of your sin and bring the blood sacrifice you will be accepted. Don't harden your heart and make things (your sin) worse. Cain still oldest could have retained his birthright. (Oldest) – Birthright –Special inheritance, rights given the firstborn son.

Verse 8

Cain is a picture of what we are by nature. It is hard to comprehend how much iniquity there is in our fallen hearts. Jeremiah 17:9 listen to Titus 3:3.

Envy and hatred are the causes of this first murder. When God approved Abel's sacrifice, Cain should have looked into his own life to find out what was wrong. Instead, his envy led him to murder. I John 3:12. We have here the first Saint to die, the first martyr.

Verse 9

Every man will give an account of his deeds. The unsaved man will before he goes to the lake of fire, the saved man will at the judgment seat.

Cain tries to cover a murder with a lie. O what folly sin brings. How could Cain think that God could not see what happened? You see sin produces arrogance and rebellion.

Verse 10

Cain thought he could silence Abel, but murder is a <u>crying sin.</u> Abel's blood had a voice. <u>Hebrews 11:4</u>.

Verse 11

Abel's blood cried out for vengeance. <u>Christ's blood cried out for pardon. Adam's curse for sin fell to the ground, Cain's curse fell upon himself</u>. We are all sinners yes, <u>but there are judgments that we bring upon ourselves</u>.

Verse 12

<u>Haggai 1:5 -7</u> – Cain was to experience disgrace among men, and a <u>haunting conscience</u>. You can never get away (geographically) from your heart. Cain had trouble, in his sustenance and settlement. He had trouble enjoying his life.

Verse 13

<u>No penitence</u>, <u>no sorrow</u>. <u>Cain pitied himself</u>. One of the consequences of sin is that it makes the sinner pity himself instead of causing him to turn to God. One of the first signs of new life is that the individual <u>takes sides with God against himself</u>.

<u>There is forgiveness with God</u>. Cain made nothing of his sin, <u>no repentance.</u> Instead of wondering why we are so mistreated, <u>we need to wonder why we are not in hell</u>. The devil would have us to go

around thinking that we are so mistreated, that God is so hard on us.

Verse 14

Cain was conscience that his sin deserved the wrath of man. Here is <u>remorse</u> NOT <u>Repentance</u>. We see here torment of mind. ("Everybody is against me.")

Verse 15

<u>God marked Cain</u>, and <u>he was known as the man who killed his brother</u>. There was no set government. Capital punishment did not come into being until after the flood.

Verse 16

Cain moves out from God, and establishes a civilization apart from God.

"Nod" – Wandering. This fulfills the prophecy of 4:12.

Remember the way of Cain is self-will. He started with human reason as opposed to divine revelation; he continued in human willfulness instead of divine will; he opposed divine humility, to human pride; he sank to human hatred instead of rising to divine love; he presented human excuses instead of seeking divine grace; he went into wandering instead of seeking to return; he ended in human loneliness instead of in divine fellowship.

Verse 17

The question so often asked for so many years is, who did Cain marry? His sister, Genesis 5:4. Listen to this comment. It is now against the law to marry your sister. Children would be deformed. Cain knew his wife. How many unbelievers have used this woman as an excuse for their departure from the Word of God! Yet Genesis 5:4 says that Adam and Eve had daughters. And if it be argued that a man may not marry his sister, we answer that a stream is purer at the source than at the mouth.

Who would not prefer to drink from the Mississippi in upper Minnesota then in New Orleans? Every generation, like cities on the banks of a stream, puts its sewage into the human race. Adam married even closer than a sister; he married his own rib! Only a man who is looking for an excuse to get away from God will be troubled by such questions as this.

Here in verse 17 we have the beginning of city life. The first civilization was founded by a murderer. Even though Cain settled down in one place he was still a wanderer at heart. He builds a city and names it after his son Enoch. Men have been doing this ever since, streets schools, building. Notice – Psalms 49:11.

We notice in Genesis 5:18 - God's Enoch/Devil's Enoch. The Godly Enoch who came from Adam through Seth the godly line.

Verse 19

Here is the beginning of <u>polygamy</u>.

Verses 23 – 24

The first murderer produced a grandson who was a murderer. The first murderer was committed in <u>envy</u> this one in <u>pride</u>. Lamech is strutting before his two wives, boasting of his <u>bloody deed</u>.

Verse 25

<u>"Seth"</u> – Means – <u>appointed</u> or <u>substituted</u>. Seth took the place of Abel. The line from which the Saviour would come was now <u>sure.</u> <u>It is impossible to destroy the plan of God.</u> Satan made war on God's plan but failed. Eve seemed to recognize that Seth was replacing Abel and not Cain.

Verse 26

Seth and his descendants developed systematic habits of prayer and <u>sacrifices</u>, enjoying Gods fellowship. The worshipers of God began to <u>distinguish themselves</u>.

Chapter 5

The generations of Adam through <u>Cain's</u> line
has been given to us and is now dropped, it is mentioned only as it crosses the godly line. <u>Chapter 5
is like walking through a cemetery.</u> <u>Genesis 2:17, I
Corinthians 15:22</u>.

Here in verse 1 we have the first mention of
<u>"book"</u> in the Old Testament. The first mention of
<u>"book"</u> in the New Testament is <u>Matthew 1:1</u>. The
first book tells of the origins of the first Adam, the
second book speaks of the origins of the last Adam.

Verse 1

The <u>"likeness"</u> was lost in the fall and is regained
in the new birth. <u>Romans 8:29</u>. The whole of the
<u>sculpturing</u>, <u>whittling</u>, <u>sand papering</u> process of the
Christian life is to this end.

Verse 2

Eve is not a name, it is a title. God's name for
the woman is Adam. She is looked upon in her husband. That is why Miss X when she marries Mr. Y
becomes Mrs. Y. It is difficult to identify a woman
apart from her husband. Who is she? Oh, her husband is Senator Smith. Who is she? Oh, she is the
girl who married the garbage collector. Women are
to lose their identity in the identity of the husband,

because marriage is a picture of the church and Christ, we lose our identity to Him.

Verse 3

Adam was created. Seth and all the sons of Adam are born after the likeness of Adam.

Verse 5

Adam died. Adam had millions of people that were from him when he died.

Verse 18

In the 4th chapter we find Enoch, who is the grandson of Adam through Cain. Now we find another Enoch who is one of the godliest men in the Bible.

God does not want the two confused, so in the book of Jude He tells about Enoch the seventh from Adam, not the third from Adam. Jude 14.

Verse 21

Methuselah was the oldest man to live. 969 years. Methuselah died the year the flood came.

Verse 24

Hebrews 11:5. Enoch is the type of the church. The rapture. Enoch, Elijah taken to heaven alive – paradise.

Verse 29

Noah – Noah undoubtedly heard the preaching of his great-grandfather Enoch.

CHAPTER 6

Verses 1 – 2

The "sons of God" were of the godly line of Seth. Genesis 4:25-26. Seth was righteous like Abel, and is through Seth and his descendants, "...then began men to call upon the name of the LORD."

Throughout the Bible saved people are called "Sons of God" or Children of God." And so we take it that the descendants of Seth are godly people like those named in chapter 5. Deuteronomy 14, Luke 3:38.

"...the daughters of men..." – not exclusive to Cain. Adam's other descendant. Cain was a wicked man, and nothing is said of his descendants serving the Lord. So they are not "sons of God" but were natural, fleshy sons of man. And so the "sons of God" refer to the line of Seth and "the daughters of men" refer to those natural unconverted woman that the sons of God married.

Angels are spoken of as sexless beings. No female angels are ever mentioned in the Bible. Marriage is unknown among angels. Matthew 22:30, Luke 20:35-36. "Like produces like."

Verse 2

Marks the breaking down of the separation between the godly line of Seth and the godless line of

Cain.

II Corinthians 6:14-18, Deuteronomy 7:1-4, I Kings 11 :1-4. And so here in Genesis 6 we have the mixing of the Sethites and the Cainites. Moral distinctions are gone, and the Sethites become badly contaminated.

Verse 3

The blessed Spirit of God strove with these men before the flood to repent, to return to God. I Peter 3:18-20. Christ was in the saving business in the Old Testament and the Holy Spirit was warning men.

"...yet his days shall be an hundred and twenty years." Noah preached for 120 years and during that time the Spirit of God was striving with men. God was long suffering in the days of Noah. The old ages of people in those days 800 – 900 years were cut down after the flood. Moses, Deuteronomy 34:7, David Psalms 90:10.

Verse 4

There were giant men in those days. Not only big, but bad, violent, lawless and deformed. There have been lingering traces of the giants down through the centuries. Some were among the Philistines like Goliath and his family. I Samuel 17:4, Deuteronomy 3:11.

Verse 5

There was not a single heart turning to God. Noah preached over 120 years without a single convert outside his own immediate family. Human eyes see the wickedness of human actions, but only God can tell what goes on in the hidden chambers of the heart. Ezekiel 11:5, Proverbs 16:2 then listen to II Corinthians 10:5.

Verse 6

Oh the grief of God as He looked on the race of man. Man was made to honor God and love him, but instead man became the enemy of God, so perverted that there are no good thoughts, no good intentions, no repenting, and no righteousness. God knows all things. Amen? Amen! And so when God said "And it repented the LORD that he had made man." Does this mean that God changed His mind? NO He is teaching that sin brings the display of His wrath.

Verse 7

Every person's breath is in the hand of God. Matthew 10:28, Numbers 21:5-9, Romans 13:3-4. Think of God's mercy at the flood, the children went to heaven, instead of growing up to be demon possessed.

Verse 8

Grace is of God. And it is always Grace first then the happy results. Another first mention – "Grace."

Verse 9

Was Noah sinless? No! He was completely sold out to God, he was sincere. He was one of the hero's of faith found in Hebrews 11:7. Note an order, Noah "found grace," then Noah was a "just man" that is justified, and so he was "perfect in his generations" he was complete, and was able to walk with God. Noah did all that God commanded him." 6:22, 7:5, 7:9, 7:16.

Verse 10 -13

Man had a promise of Redeemer, he was told there was a coming Saviour. This is what man should have been looking for, instead he turned from God. The earth was corrupt, the earth was filled with violence, and all flesh had corrupted his way. Shem, Ham and Japheth, escaped the corruption. Had it not been for the example and teachings of their godly parents and grandparents, no doubt they to would have lived wicked lives. I want to point out that it helped them when their father had them busy building the ark.

Notice in verse 12 – "And God looked upon the earth ..." although the earth had forgotten God, God was still looking on the earth. Hebrews 4:13.

Verse 14

What faith. What if God told you to build an 18,000 ton ship? When God commands the impossible, He will supply the faith.

One of the greatest acts of faith in the history of the world was when Noah stretched out his hand and grasped the first tool to build the Ark.

<u>Pitch</u> – Pitch is the same Hebrew word for <u>atonement</u>. <u>Leviticus 17:11</u> There can be no leak in the Ark, it is the <u>pitch</u> that keeps the <u>waters</u> from entering, or <u>judgment</u> from entering. The judgment of God can never touch the believer because the death of the Lord Jesus Christ stands between him and the wrath of God forever.

Verse 17

For the <u>first time God</u> tells Noah exactly what form the coming destruction would be.

Verse 18

<u>First mention</u> of <u>"covenant."</u> <u>Details</u> of covenant found in <u>Genesis 9:9-17</u>.

Verse 22

Just think any disobedience on Noah's part and the ark would have been dangerous. <u>90% obedience</u> is <u>disobedience</u>. That would not have been good enough. <u>"Thus did Noah; according to all that God commanded him, so did he."</u>

CHAPTER 7

Verse 1

"And the LORD said unto Noah, Come..." – What a tender invitation. God did not command Noah to go into the ark, he invited him to.

What is the work of God? John 6:29. "...for thee have I seen righteous before me..." Beauty is in the eyes of the beholder. In ourselves there is no loveliness, but God has designed to look upon us through the Lord Jesus Christ.

A child may have a broken toy but would rather play with it then any other toy, why? Because of something in the heart of the child. The Lord found us righteous before Him because of something in His heart. And that something is what He has seen in Christ who is made unto us righteousness. I Corinthians 1:30.

Verses 2-3

The clean animals were no doubt to be used for sacrificial offerings. Seven to ensure a good number for future development.

Verse 4-5

Seven days. This could be to give Noah time for last minute preparations to enter the ark. God miraculously controlled the situation in gathering up all the animals and leading them to go into the ark.

We see faith in Noah as he obeys the Lord and enters the ark. During these seven days with the ark done and the flood about to come, people could have entered the ark, they could have believed.

Verse 6-10

Noah must have paused and had <u>solemn thoughts</u> as he entered the ark, <u>realizing the coming doom upon all the people</u>. He had to be thinking of people in <u>Hell</u>! We see the end of the <u>antediluvian</u> age. Antediluvian - People who lived before the flood.

Verse 11-12

The flood came on the earth <u>1655 years, one month and seventeen days after creation</u>.

We have the "<u>waters above</u> the <u>firmament</u>" and "waters <u>below</u> the <u>firmament.</u>" The <u>waters above</u> the <u>firmament</u> made a <u>vaporous canopy</u>, which made the earth as a <u>greenhouse</u>, preventing cold temperatures and wind and rain. The <u>waters below</u> the <u>firmament</u> were <u>"the great deep."</u> So we have the waters below <u>bursting their bounds</u> and the waters above <u>falling in torrential rains.</u>

Verse 13-16

<u>The Lord shut the door. What a picture of salvation.</u> The ark pictures Jesus Christ the <u>"ark of safety."</u> One who is in Christ is safe. The shutting in of Noah

is the equivalent of our being sealed with the Holy Spirit. Ephesians 4:30. Noah was not only saved he was safe and secure.

Verse 17-24

The same waters that destroyed life on earth bore up the ark and Noah and his family were safe. Noah was on the ark for over a year. Man cannot escape God's judgment. Obadiah 3-4.

CHAPTER 8

Verse 1-2

"And God remembered Noah..." – This does not mean that God forgot Noah, it means, - began again to act on their behalf. God took action in three ways. 1. He caused a wind to pass over the earth. 2. He stopped the fountains of the deep from further eruptions. 3. He closed the windows of heaven from further downpours. Notice – Psalms 104:6-9.

Verse 3-4

The ark rested. This is the second time the mention of rest is found in scripture. The first is when God rested after His work of creation. Genesis 2:2-3. God's judgment has been executed.

Verse 5-12

Noah released a raven and a dove from the ark. The dove returned, but the raven, a scavenger bird had no problem resting on unclean surfaces. A week later, Noah sent out the dove again, which returned this time with an olive leaf. Then Noah sent out the dove again. This time the dove stayed, which meant land was dry. Verses 13-14

Verse 15-19

A little more than a year earlier God said to Noah in 7:1. Now God says, "Go forth of the ark..."

Jesus says to us "Come unto me…" then He says, "Go ye into all the world, and preach the gospel…" Oh how different it was for Noah and his family now as they come off the ark. Everything was so different. Isn't that true when you get saved? Amen!

Verse 20

Now that Noah is on dry land his thoughts turn to God. Ever since Eden, the way of access to God had been through animal sacrifice, thru blood. We are saved by the blood of Jesus and our fellowship is maintained by the blood of Jesus.

This is the first mention of "altar" in scripture. (God First).

Verse 21

"And the LORD smelled a sweet savour…" The Lord was pleased with the believing prayer of Noah. We all have benefited from Noah's sacrifice of intercession, and God's response to it. God promised that He would never again send a world wide flood.

"…for the imagination of man's heart *is* evil from his youth…" We see here the love and grace of God. We see the Original sin and universal depravity, and also Gods redeeming mercy.

Noah offers animal sacrifices and so did Abel they understood that the sacrifice represented Christ, the Lamb of God who would come and die. Those who were saved in the Old Testament times were saved by faith in the Saviour who would come. Dimly it may be they saw, but by faith they did see that God would provide a sacrifice, Genesis 22:8, Hebrews 11:14. Today we take the Lord's Supper, the memorial supper picturing the death of Christ for us. The sacrificial Lamb meant the same to Noah, although the sacrifice pictured was in the future.

Verse 22

"While the earth remaineth..." This promise would be as long as the earth remainith. That is until God burns this earth, but not until the day of the Lord comes.

I Peter 3:10. The effects of the curse will be removed. There will always be four seasons. Until the end.

CHAPTER 9

Verse 1

Adam is the head of the race, Noah in a way is the head of the <u>new beginning. This is a new start and it is marked with God's blessings. God in his holiness and hatred of sin had manifested His judgment upon the sin of the world.</u> God is with Noah and is in their new beginning. <u>God went with them through the flood and now will be with them in the new life that begins</u>.

God gives them the command for fruitfulness. To fill the earth, yes, but also to obey Him in this new opportunity.

Verse 2

God had given Adam domain over all the animals. Now God assures Noah of his safety by putting the fear and dread of man into the heart of the animals.

Verse 3

<u>Now God says that meat is good for eating.</u> Noah was a vegetarian before the flood. Now with the change of weather, animals were important not only for food but for clothing.

Verse 4

The blood of animals was figurative to cover sins, the blood was not to be consumed.

Verse 5-6

Before the flood there was <u>no organized human government</u>. Now we have the <u>death penalty</u>. Cain was allowed to go with a mark upon him so no one would kill him. <u>But now there will be a rule of human government</u>. <u>Verse 6</u>. We see this carried over into the ceremonial law, and expanded. <u>Exodus 21:12-17, Romans 13:4</u>.

Verse 7

A repetition of God's instructions in verse 1.

Verse 8-10

<u>Noahic covenant</u>, <u>rainbow covenant</u>. This covenant is not only with Noah and his descendants <u>but</u> also with the animals going out of the ark. Animals are part of God's creation.

Verse 11

This is <u>God's promise</u>. <u>His purpose</u> is that He will not again destroy the earth with a flood. The next time His judgment of the earth will be by fire. <u>II Peter 3</u>.

Verse 12-13

The rainbow is a <u>token</u> of a covenant. <u>Hebrews 6:17</u> – a <u>seal</u>.

Verse 14-17

God will never send a <u>universal flood</u>. When

THE BOOK OF BEGINNINGS

they would see the rainbow after a rain their fears would go away. "Repeated assurances." "God's eye of grace and our eye of faith meet in the rainbow covenant."

Verse 18-29

Everybody in the world is descended from these son's of Noah. We have a first mention here in verse 21 – "wine." It is here associated with drunkenness and shame. Noah was not ignorant of the wine being fermented. Noah had stood strong for God for many, many, many years, now he let down his guard. Scripture warns us in I Peter 5:8. Satan had been unable to corrupt the family of Noah before the flood. Noah got drunk and took off his clothes and lay sleeping naked. Ham entered the tent and was surprised to see his father lying there naked and in a drunken sleep. He did more than see, he gazed. I don't believe he committed a homosexual act. Ham rejoiced at his father's sin, and told his brothers with delight. Shem and Japheth reacted quite differently. I Peter 4:8. Ham's sin was not only against his father but against God.

Ham, Canaan - Noah's prophecy of this carnal, materialistic nature.

Noah lived to see two worlds.

Prophetic declarations concerning Noah's sons:

1. Ham – Upon Ham through his son Canaan

God placed a curse and decreed that, "a servant of servants shall he be unto his brethren..." Genesis 9:22, 24, 25.

2. Shem – A blessing was pronounced. Genesis 9:26. Through Shem comes the "seed of the woman." The line of Christ. All Israel comes through Shem.

3. Japheth – God promises to enlarge Japheth. Genesis 9:27. From Japheth comes all Gentile Nations.

CHAPTER 10

First we see the genealogy of <u>Japheth</u>. <u>Verses 2 – 5</u>. <u>Ham</u>, <u>verses 6 – 20</u>. <u>Shem</u>, <u>verses 21 – 32</u>. <u>Here we have the beginnings of the nations.</u>

Verse 2

Gentile Nations

Verse 6

The curse was only upon <u>Canaan</u>. From Canaan came the <u>Hittites,</u> the <u>Jebusites,</u> the <u>Amonites,</u> the <u>Girgashites,</u> and the <u>Hirites.</u> Enemies of <u>God's people.</u>

Verse 8-9

Here we have the beginning of human <u>dictatorship.</u> <u>Nimrod</u> was a <u>hunter of men's souls.</u>

Verse 10

He was the lawless one and he is a shadow or a type of the last world ruler. <u>The Antichrist.</u>

In chapter 10 seventy nations are listed, <u>14</u> from Japheth, <u>30</u> from Ham and <u>26</u> from Shem.

Verse 25

<u>Continental drift</u> or from <u>Babel</u>? Which <u>describes</u> the <u>coming division</u>?

CHAPTER 11

Verse 1-3

The thought of every action is whether it comes from the <u>will of man</u> or from <u>the will of God</u>. <u>Man</u> in <u>rebellion</u> says, <u>"Let us,"</u> man in <u>submission</u> says, <u>"Thy will be done."</u>

Verse 4

God's command was to replenish the earth. <u>Must scatter for that.</u>

Verse 5

Not only does the Lord know all that is going on in the earth, but he is interested in all that takes place.

Verse 6

They wanted to dwell together so that they would have <u>strength</u> to do <u>their own will</u>.

Verse 7

<u>The Lord confounded their language</u>. <u>Pentecost was a witness to the Grace of God</u>. <u>One day at His coming we will be united in our language</u>.

Verse 8-9

<u>God always has His way in the end.</u> It is impossible that the eternal council's of the <u>God head should not be fulfilled</u>. It is always best to get in on God's

program. There is no real peace for you and me until
we do.

Verse 27-32

God appeared to Abram and gave the orders.
Well because of Terah they landed and stayed in
Haran a while. But then Terah died.

CHAPTER 12

The <u>Covenant</u> included three basic provisions,

1. Land – territory later outlined in <u>Genesis.</u>

2. A Great Nation – would multiply as the sand of the sea.

3. A Blessing – that would affect all nations – "<u>Promised Christ</u>" in <u>Galatians 3:16.</u> The blessing primarily spiritual in nature, all people can reap the benefits of the Abrahamic Covenant through Christ. Jesus has been a blessing in many ways. Education, political, scientific and doctrinal.

<u>Fringe benefits</u>, God's blessings upon any nation that would bless, show kindness toward Abraham's descendants. <u>Psalms 122:6.</u>

<u>Genesis 1-11</u> deals with events primarily. Now beginning in chapter 12 we begin to see important <u>personalities</u> as primary focus. <u>The human race.</u>

While in Haran God renewed His call to Abram given to Abram earlier.

<u>Acts 7:2-3</u>, to go into the land of Canaan to establish the new nation. According to <u>Joshua 24:2.</u> Terah had begun to worship other gods while still in Chaldea. So the call came once again to Abram and he obeyed without further delay.

Verse 1-3

<u>Abram's covenant.</u> <u>God made to Abram a won-</u>

derful promise. He told him He would establish a great nation through him, a nation through which someday all other nations would be blessed. We have a statement of faith, verses 1-3.

We have a step of faith in verse 4. This promise is one of the first promises of the Coming Saviour, who would bring salvation to all nations. God had long ago made it clear that the Saviour would be born into a human family. (Seed of the woman). Genesis 3:15. And now here in chapter 12 it becomes clear to Abram that it would be accomplished through his own family.

God promised protection, saying He would bless those that blessed Abram and curse those that curse Him.

The Jewish nation has been blessed and protected in a marvelous way through the centuries.

Verse 2

"And I will make of thee a great nation..." This is one of the first unconditional promises. The promise is not because of what Abram is or can do, but because of God's grace and His plan, because of who He is. We see unmerited grace here, "I will bless thee." II Timothy 2:13. We know all the failures of Abraham, Jacob, David, etc... but that doesn't change the plan of God.

Verse 4

We see Abraham's obedience to the Lord. <u>Hebrews 11:8</u>. Abraham was <u>75 years old</u>, Sarai was <u>65 years</u>. The aging process was still much slower than it is in our day. Verse 11.

<u>Lot believed God</u>. Something in the faith and life of his uncle Abraham rubbed off on him. Lot was not as strong as Abraham; he would cause Abraham a lot of trouble.

Verse 5

When Abram stepped out on his travels it was the <u>proof that he believed the promise of God</u>. It was a long journey to Canaan, about 400 miles.

Verse 6

The journey was tough for Abram. The Canaanite's were the descendants of Ham. The terrain, and the heathen people made it tough journey for Abram.

Verse 7

<u>This is the first time we have a stated appearance of God</u>. God had <u>walked</u>, and <u>spoken</u> to <u>Adam</u>, <u>Enoch</u> and <u>Noah,</u> and perhaps He also had been visible in some way to them. <u>Here is a theophany</u> – a <u>pre-Bethlehem appearance of Christ</u>.

There are many trials and struggles and blessings in our walk here on earth. <u>New supplies of Grace</u>

will meet us at every point of conflict.

The Lord confirmed His promise to Abram. Blessed Assurance Jesus is mine, O what a fore taste of glory divine.

"Thy seed" Abram's seed. 1. The seed as the dust of the earth, that Israel the race, and promise to inherit the land of Israel. 2. The seed as the stars for multitude, all the spiritual seed, like him saved by faith. 3. The great seed, which is Christ.

In the place of the appearance of the presence of God stood the altar. Abram builds an altar for there is worship and communion that goes with the promise of God.

Verse 8

A tent and an alter, this was all that Abram had. He was what is called a Nomad, but he was walking with God and teaching us that the life of faith is subject to change without notice. As long as we have the altar and our tent we have all that is necessary, a promise. God's word.

Verse 10

Here we have a severe trial of Abram's faith. A grievous famine came and it looked as though the land could no longer sustain him and his family and flocks. God's promise had not changed. Abram needs to learn to trust God. Abram was not equal to this test; he soon yielded to the temptation to take matters into his own hand. God told him to go to Canaan where He would bless him, <u>but</u> now it seemed that Canaan was no longer able to support him. The land of Egypt was prosperous and so Abram made the decision without <u>calling on God for guidance</u> to move to Egypt.

God had not brought Abram all this way to let him die of hunger. <u>Oh how we need to learn to walk by faith</u>.

At times the walk with God will be such that even faith will hardly know where to turn. The question is – <u>"Can we be satisfied with God, can we trust God?"</u>

Verse 11-16

<u>One failure leads to another</u>. Abram goes down to Egypt and then finds himself with a decision to make that he was not planning on. <u>As Abram entered the mighty land of Egypt he became aware of danger</u>. The Egyptians were immoral and Abram noticed the admiring looks of the Egyptians towards his beautiful wife Sarai. <u>So he made a decision to have Sarai say she was his sister, instead of her husband, because he reasoned they would kill him for Sarai.</u> But if she was his sister they would treat him good. <u>Sarai in truth was his half-sister</u>. Genesis 20:12. A <u>half truth is a lie.</u> <u>Amen!</u> Abram who had walked by faith all the way from <u>UR</u> to <u>Canaan,</u>

began to walk by the circumstances of the famine. And so having forgotten the counsel and care of the Lord, he forgot the promise of God concerning the seed which was to come. Abram allowed his wife to go into the Palace of Ham, where if it had not been for the intervention of God, her womb might have been contaminated.

It all turned out better than they had hoped. Sarai was so beautiful that she was brought to the attention of Pharaoh himself instead of just ordinary Egyptians. Not only did Pharaoh's princes notice Sarai's physical beauty but also her inner beauty. I Peter 3:3-6.

Verse 17

Thank God for His intervention in their lives. Sarah was to be the mother of the faithful. She was a free woman, a type of salvation by grace. Galatians 4:22-24.

Verse 18-20

Abram suffered the shame and humiliation of a man, who having been an ambassador for God, was sent away like a dog with his tail between his legs. It was not a pretty sight but the effects of sin are never pretty. Pharaoh could have said of Abram, "if that is Christianity, I don't need it."

CHAPTER 13

Verse 1

Our God is the God of the second opportunity, and of the 82nd opportunity. We can begin fresh with the God of Grace.

We often go down into Egypt and God always waits for us to return. He creates difficulties for us in Egypt so that we may long for the grapes of His land and the blessings of His communion. The Devils, swine husks or the fathers fatted calf. The choice is ours.

The only way to get back into the will of God is to go back to the very place of departure, confess it, forsake it, and return to the place of fellowship. Repentance for salvation, for fellowship.

Verse 1-4

As they traveled up from Egypt they did not stop until they reached once again, Bethel, the last place where Abram had built an altar and called on the name of the Lord. God promises to forgive our sins when we confess them. I John 1:9.

Verse 5

Abram had flocks but the flocks did not have him. Lot had flocks and the flocks possessed him. It is a terrible thing when a Christian is possessed by his possessions.

The <u>love</u> of money is the <u>root</u> of <u>all evil.</u> <u>I Timothy 6:10</u>.

Lot is in heaven, because he was <u>justified</u>. <u>II Peter 2:7</u>. Lot is the father of all tight fisted money loving people who put <u>things before God</u>. Lot's story is a sad story of loss. <u>He was saved yet so as by fire with all his works burned away.</u> <u>I Corinthians 3:15</u>. Since it is possible to be in heaven with loss. <u>I Corinthians 9:27, Revelation 3:11</u>. God exhorts us to take heed and beware.

Verse 6

Abram obeys a great principal found in <u>Philippians 2:4</u> "<u>Look not every man on his own things, but every man also on the things of others.</u>" This is the unselfish thing to do, and shows that the life of Christ is within. <u>It was his by promise.</u> (Land) When this scene is over we find that God visited Abram and renewed His promise to Abram. When ever a believer will behave in this God given way, <u>he/she</u> will be amply rewarded both here and there. <u>God will bless.</u>

"<u>Dwell together.</u>" There would be enough land to take care of the need if Abram and Lot <u>separated</u>. This separation, which should have taken place in <u>12:1</u> Ur of the Chaldee's now takes place.

Verse 7

The experience of Abram going down into Egypt no doubt left scars on Lot. <u>Lot was self seeking</u>, and no doubt the experience of <u>seeing Egypt with all its</u> <u>wealth aggravated their situation</u>. Oh how important material possessions are to some. This friction was a bad testimony to the <u>Canaanites</u> and the <u>Perizzites or the world.</u>

Verse 8

It takes two to quarrel. Abram was willing to give in, <u>even when he was right</u>. (All the land was his anyway). Abram won. The only right we have is to go to Hell.

<u>I Corinthians 6:19-20, 7:23</u>.

Verse 9

Abram has learned that God could take care of his needs no matter where he was, so He offered Lot the choice. Abram was the senior and should have had first choice. <u>We see his spirit of sacrifice.</u>

Verse 10

Lot seized the opportunity to his own advantage (so he thought). He had been infected with the luxury and excitement of Egypt, and was no longer <u>content</u> to be a stranger and pilgrim in the land. Lot's eyes were the binoculars of his heart that day he looked upon the <u>plains of Jordan</u>. <u>Lot made a fatal choice that day</u>. <u>II Corinthians 4:18.</u>

Those who see only the earthly springs do not realize how quickly these springs dry up. <u>John 7:38</u>.

The man who learns that all his springs are in the Lord need never fear the desert, <u>because</u> He carries with him his own <u>irrigation system.</u>

Verse 11

The humility, kindness and generosity of Abram did not melt Lot. His <u>heart was like a stone</u>. His greedy heart would not be moved. Abram became the father of all the faithful, Lot became the father of all the <u>compromisers</u>.

Verse 12

One step out of the will of God always leads to another. Lot first <u>"...pitched *his* tent toward Sodom."</u> but soon <u>dwelt in Sodom</u>, <u>14:12</u>, and finally <u>"sat in the gate of Sodom"</u> as one of its business leaders, <u>19:1.</u>

<u>"Abram dwelled in the land of Canaan..."</u> the land of promise.

Verse 13

Lot knew about the wickedness of Sodom. It was well known.

The most terrible thing about sin is that it is sin before the Lord. A sinful act hurts the person and those around him, but it <u>hurts the Lord most</u>. <u>David</u> knew this well in <u>Psalms 51:4</u>.

This ought to make us think about sin.

<u>God sees</u>, <u>Hebrews 4:13.</u>

Verse 14

Now that Abram was separated from Lot, he could devote his full attention to serving God and walking In His will. <u>Abram was a friend of God.</u> <u>James 2:23</u>, the Lord could now talk to him freely. Within our hearts as Christians we have the struggle of <u>Abram and Lot</u>, <u>the spiritual and the carnal</u>, it is only when the carnal departs, that faith receives the <u>place of affection</u>. Then God reveals to us His desires for our fellowship with Him.

God's arithmetic – 1+1= everything. When you surrender to God, you have everything.

<u>"Lift up now thine eyes..."</u> Lot may have had a better land, <u>but</u> Abram had the <u>title deed</u>, Lot had his little paradise, <u>but</u> Abram had the promise.

This place of separation becomes a place of vision. We may find ourselves in the middle of a struggle that we think will over come us. <u>But when we yield to Him and are separate from all that would keep us from the Heavenly Wisdom, we shall find glory in the valley of struggle.</u>

We once again see God's grace as He confirms His covenant with Abram.

Verse 15

Abram had the promise but never actually possessed it all in his lifetime. As far as Israel owning all of what was promised, it seems to be yet future.

During the Millennium there will then be full possession. Right now we have untold promises of God
which we have not explained. We believe them in
His word and when we want to begin to possess
them. <u>He will make them good</u>.

Verse 16

God assured Abram <u>again</u> that He would make
him a great nation, with his seed numbering, "<u>...as
the dust of the earth...</u>" or enumerable.

We are talking not only of the <u>physical descen-
dants</u> but also <u>the spiritual</u>. <u>Galatians 3:16</u>, from
Abram's seed came Christ. Abram is father of all the
faithful, <u>Romans 4:11</u>, spiritual seed.

Verse 17

The land became Abram's as he possessed it.
<u>Deuteronomy 11:24</u>, the land was theirs in the
measure of their occupation of it. You see it was all
Abram's and his seed by right and title, but when he
walked around an acre, he possessed an acre, when
he walked around a mile, he possessed a mile. When
he climbed a hill, the hill was his etc... So it is for
us with all the promises of God. We are to possess
the promises from <u>Genesis to Revelation</u>. Wherever
we plant our feet in possession, the promise will become ours.

Verse 18

As we close chapter 13 we find Abram a much wiser man <u>by experience</u>. He first pitched his tent at Bethel, <u>House of God</u>, and built an alter there. He then went through the Egypt experience. He dwells in Mamre and pitches his ten in Hebron. <u>And builds an alter there</u>. It is impossible to walk with God without gaining greater knowledge of Him, and experience more wonderful communion with Him. <u>Proverbs 4:18, Philippians 1:6</u>. Abram is now a <u>true pilgrim</u>. When he removed his tent and pitched it in Hebron, he built an alter, giving thanks to God.

CHAPTER 14

Chapter 14 records the first battle in the Bible, and in all of recorded history. There are also first mentions of Priest, Kings, bread, wine and tithes. We have here God's idea of King Priest in Melchizedek. Hebrews 7:1-4. Picture of God, Kingdom, Priesthood.

Verse 1-4

What we have here is a confederation of kings. These kingdoms were small. This area of battle was in the area of the Dead Sea.

Verse 5-12

All sides around the Dead Sea were invaded for the gain of power and territory.

King Cherdorlaomer's armies gathered up all the possessions of the cities, including the women, children, servants and others. Unfortunately for him, he also took Lot and his family. Lot was living in Sodom and was carnal, but he was a "righteous man." II Peter 2:8

Verse 12-13

Lot first pitched his tent toward Sodom, and then came to dwell in Sodom. There is only one way to victory, complete separation.

Abram dwelt in Mamre, vision and communion.

He was untroubled by the wars between these kings.
All of this was a great concern to Lot, because he
was dwelling where he had no business to be. Lot
was suffering for his bad choices.

Verse 14

Abram could have said, "It serves him right; he
has it coming to him." The man of God is not that
way. Spiritual men are in the business of restoration.
When a Christian is yielded to God he/she cannot
have the root of bitterness.

"Trained servants." Abram was not a pacifist; he
lived in the midst of wars and rumors of wars. He
trained his men and was ready.

Verse 13-16

Abram by this time was practically a king himself. Verse 14, "318 men" all of them trained. This
number was no match for all of the invading armies.
This reminds us of the odds against Gideon who
with 300 battled against 135,000 Midianites. Judges
8:10. God was with Abram as He was with Gideon,
and that was more than enough.

Verse 17-24

We have here the encounter of Abram and
Melchizedek King of Salem. He was mentioned
hundreds of years later by Daniel and Paul. Psalms
110:4, Hebrews 5:6,10, 6:20 and 7:1-21.

Some people would have had their heads turned by recognition from a king. <u>But not Abram</u>. When John Knox was asked if he were frightened by the prospect of meeting the Queen of Scotland, he replied that he had just spent <u>four hours with God.</u> Such a man can't be impressed by a mere Queen.

Abram gladly recognized Melchizedek as representing the same God who had called him to Canaan. Abram recognized Melchizedek as his spiritual superior, and gave him <u>title of all</u>.

Verse 18-19

"And he blessed him…" At the end of a day of battle, the Lord comes with His provision.

Bread, wine – Picture of our Precious Saviour, His cross – broken body and spilt blood.

CHAPTER 15

Verse 1

"After these things…" Every day is a new begin-ning with God. After failure we can begin a fresh with Him. After success we need to begin with Him. We need to forget what lies behind, and go on for God. Philippians 3:13.

"…the word of the LORD came unto Abram…" This is the first time that the well known phrase is found in scripture. The Word of God is living and powerful. Hebrew 4:12. The Word of God will al-ways produce what God has purposed it to. Isaiah 55:11.

"Fear not, Abram…" Fear is a natural part of our make-up as humans. After all the excitement Abram had experienced saving Lot by going out against four Kings and then the wonderful experience with Melchizedek. After everyone had gone and Abram was alone, he began to think, and began to be a bit doubtful and fearful of what the future might hold. "Fear not," came to him. Oh the comfort of the Word of the Lord.

"…I *am* thy shield…" The man who defeats the enemy becomes a target. The Kings could regroup, but God comes to Abram with assurance. "…I *am* thy shield…" the Lord always provides the armor for His people, and that armor is Himself. Satan confessed to God that he had to turn back from Job because of the hedge of God. Job 1:10. The whole armor of God. Ephesians 6:11, has been provided, and our enemies must break through God Himself to reach us. Colossians 3:3.

"...thy exceeding great reward." No one ever lost anything by giving up something for God. The Lord has never remained in debt to anyone. The Lord comes to those who put their trust in Him, and provides for all their needs. Philippians 4:19 Matthew 19:27-29 II Chronicles 13:13-18.

Verse 2

Ten years has come and gone since Abram arrived in the land. The promise of his being made a great nation was becoming dim. He was old. Abram and Sarah were beyond the age of child bearing. Things were not encouraging and Abram spread it all out before the Lord. Even when we have the promise and are unwilling to wait for its fulfillment. God is kind and gracious to us.

In verses 2 and 3, Abram is saying "I don't have a son yet." His steward by law would inherit if Abram had no son.

Verse 4

God did not chew out Abram for his lack of faith. I Corinthians 13:4, "Charity suffereth long, *and* is kind..." Psalms 103:14. God was saying "I am going to give you a son." God loves to encourage us, and comes to us when we feel like fainting.

Verse 5

God reassures Abram of the promise. <u>Genesis 12:2, 13:16, 15:5, 22:17.</u> Abram understood about his seed. <u>John 8:56.</u> His physical seed, Israel. Spiritual seed, Church. <u>Galatians 3:29</u>.

Verse 6

<u>First mention "believed."</u> Abram believed God and He counted or imputed it to him for righteousness. Here is the great principle of <u>free salvation</u>. <u>Not by works do men attain righteousness, but by faith</u>. This wonderful verse is quoted three times in the New Testament. <u>Romans 4:3, Galatians 3:6, James 2:23.</u>

Verse 7

Abram has become discouraged. God's delays are never denials. He gives us a promise and wants us to grow in it. When we learn the first lesson, He will teach us the second. We don't teach algebra before learning the multiplication table.

It would be several more years before Isaac would be born, but now Abram was resting in faith. God reminds him that He is working with a definite purpose.

Verse 8

Abram asked this question out of a heart of faith. He was asking to be more clearly informed. Luke 1:18-20.

Verse 9-11

The curse of sin can be removed only by sacrifice, in the shedding of blood. Abram knew this, God was stressing the connection of sacrifice with the promise. After Abram made the preparations, nothing happened the rest of the day. This may be a picture of the fact that although God's promise would be sure, it would take a long time. Abram would have to wait yet many years before he received his son. And the nation would wait many, many long centuries before the seed would become a great nation and possess the Promised Land.

During the wait Abram had to drive off the birds of prey. This is a picture of Satan attempting to throw cold water on God's plan.

Verse 12-21

This symbolizes the long tribulation of Israel in Egypt. Verse 17 represents God's presence in the covenantal relation with Abram. Verse 18, the covenant already made, is now expounded on.

CHAPTER 16

Verse 1

Abram and Sarai acted in unbelief. <u>A promise made to Abram was a promise made to Sarai, a man's wife is one with him in the eyes of God.</u> Abram was 85 years old and Sarai was 75. We see here a great lesson for Christians. Abram was justified by faith, but he tried to do something in his own strength, and that is a no, no. <u>God is seeking to bring us to realize our utter nothingness,</u> in order that we may utterly depend upon Him. Abram like us needs to learn to look to God.

Verse 2

<u>"... Abram hearkened to the voice of Sarai."</u> And this was a serious mistake. <u>Remember Adam in Genesis 3:17</u>? Abram had not fully learned what we read in <u>Hebrews 6:12, 10:35-36</u>. If we like Sarai get impatient and try to help God do something by human means, we will find ourselves in trouble.

Verse 3

Their trouble from before presents a tool for the devil to use. Hagar was probably acquired when Abram and Sarai went down into Egypt. Hagar was Sarai's personal property, and so any children Hagar might have would legally belong to Sarai. <u>James 1:13</u>. Notice what we have here; <u>1.</u> Sarai is barren. <u>2.</u>

Hagar was at hand. 3. Sarai urged him on. 4. Abram was a man with earth's passions.

Problems were to come. God's purpose is one man, one woman, one lifetime. There has never been and never will be a happy polygamous marriage.

Verse 4

Hagar realized that she was a woman fulfilling the functions of womanhood while Sarai remained barren. And so there was pride. Proverbs 16:18. And so you can hear Hagar say, "I've mothered a child of Abram, and Sarai couldn't do it." Hagar looked down on Sarai.

Verse 5

God did not approve of this; Sarai sees that she was wrong. It is going to be heartache to old Abram.

Verse 6

Abram was caught between these two women. All he could do was turn Hagar, which belonged to Sarai, back to her. Hagar experiences the Grace of God. Humiliation and slavery led her to God. God gives Grace to whom He will.

Verse 7

The God who sought out Adam when he had sinned now finds Hagar. God is more interested in us than we are of ourselves. This was an appearance of the Lord Jesus Christ.

We are in the wilderness of this world but our stay is the Word of God. <u>Ephesians 5:26.</u>

Verse 8

Hagar was Abram's wife, yet the Lord said, <u>"... Hagar, Sarai's maid..."</u> He said this to humble her. He asked the question for a purpose, to bring her to herself, <u>a reality check.</u> Just as we read in <u>John 4</u>. She was wrong in running away.

Verse 9

If we seek to change our circumstances, we will jump from the frying pan into the fire. We must get the victory right where we are. It is not a change in geography that we need; it is a change of heart. <u>The flesh wants to run away,</u> but God wants to demonstrate His <u>power to us right where our greatest challenge is.</u> Life's disappointments become His appointments. When we come to the end of ourselves <u>that is when we see God</u>. It may be humiliating to return to the place of failure, but that is where His power will enable us to gain the victory.

Verse 10

God did not approve of Abram and Hagar. He sent her back as Sarai's maid not Abram's wife. But He sends her back with a great promise. Her seed will be multiplied. He says <u>"Return, submit, then comes the blessings."</u>

Verse 11

Ishmael means – "God hears." And so Ishmael by his name would always remind his mother how the God of Abram (not her gods in Egypt) had met her need.

Tears speak as well as prayers. God is attentive to the cry of those who are in distress. Nothing can touch us that does not touch Him.

A promise of a son given to this Egyptian woman. Oh how Gracious God is!

Verse 12

Here is the first indication of the far reaching effects of the sin of Abram. Ishmael – Arabs of today. They are the great opponents of Israel. The father of the faithful had begotten a wild man, instead of a child of grace. This is God's judgment on self-effort.

Verse 13

Hagar learned that all, which happened to her, was known to the Heavenly Father who was interested in her cries. She had seen that God was able to meet her need. In our wilderness there is a fountain of water, verse 7. God is able.

Verse 14

The meaning of this well is "The well of the Living One who seeth me. "He that sees all sees me."

Verse 15-16

Hagar returned in obedience to God. She told Abram how that the Lord revealed to her the name of the baby. <u>And so it was</u>.

CHAPTER 17

Verse 1

"99 years old" It is never too late for God. What is age to the eternal One? Just think the work begun in us is to be performed, not till we are old and feeble, not until we die, but until the day of Jesus Christ. Philippians 1:6.

Now when God appeared again to Abram he was 99 years old. He and Sarai were now past the age for children. God revealed Himself this time to Abram by a new name, El Shaddia – Almighty God, stressing His omnipotence. God had already made His covenant with Abram. He was now ready to put it into force.

The Lord appeared to Abram again, again and again. God is teaching us. (He tells us these things were written for us, Romans 4:23-24), that He will come to us with fresh supplies of grace for every need and for our development and growth. Nothing can cause us to grow except knowledge of our Father, which is obtained through His Word.

This is not the day of visions and divine appearance any more than Abram's day was a day of the written Bible. What a great advantage we have in possessing the Holy Spirit who dwells within us, and teaches us through the Word of God.

God admonishes Abram to be careful to walk

in fellowship with Him.(as he had forgotten in the past). God never demands anything that He has not already provided. The believer must draw on the resources that have been made available.

Verse 2

God again promised to make Abram a father of many nations. <u>All blessings begin with God</u>, the One who blesses and all promises come from Him. And what He has promised, He is able to perform.

God never does anything in halves. His blessings are <u>exceedingly</u>. When He pours blessings into our cup it always overflows. Our God even increases our capacity to hold more.

Verse 3

<u>"And Abram fell on his face ..."</u> The realization of a great promise will always put us on our face before God.

God saves us, <u>we thank Him</u>, this thanksgiving pleases Him, He blesses us more, we bow before Him, He blesses us exceedingly, and we fall on our faces.

<u>"...God talked with him ..."</u> Whenever God talks, we are to listen.

Verse 4

It is promised to Abram that he should be a father of many nations. <u>Both physical and spiritual seed.</u> "Abram" means "exalted father."

Verse 5

"Abraham" the father of a multitude. "...have I made thee". Abraham was a made man, when he came to the end of himself, God, Almighty God, El Shaddai is the source of all power.

Verse 6

After God says, "... have I made thee". verse 5, He says "I will make ... thee ..." That is Gods way. Promise precedes performance, when we lay hold on the promise, we lay hold upon God. God wants to touch us to get our eyes off ourselves, and get them upon Him.

Verse 7

This was an everlasting covenant. That means it is still good today. God has given to us everlasting life through Jesus Christ. Amen. If God is not going to make good on His promise, His covenant with Abraham, then you and me friend are in big trouble. God has and will make good on all that He promises.

Verse 8

When the Giver is more to us than the gift, we shall have Him and with Him all the gifts. Matthew 6:33.

Verse 9

Grace calls for faithfulness. The love of Christ

must constrain us to live unto Him who died for us. II Corinthians 5:14.

Listen to I Corinthians 4:2-4. I am not responsible for fruit, God gives the increase. I am responsible to be faithful.

Verse 10

God here established a visible seal and sign of His covenant relation with Abraham's physical seed. This is the first use of the word circumcised. Romans 4:11, shows us that salvation came to Abraham years before he was circumcised, which shows us that there is no saving merit in circumcision.

Verse 11

God wants His people to be marked off from the world. Just as the Passover was replaced by the Lord's Supper, so circumcision was replaced by baptism. Colossians 2:11-12. Baptism cannot save any more than circumcision.

Verse 12

Our children are our most important possession; they must be marked from the Lord and for the Lord from their earliest days. This obligation was not only for the children born of Abraham, but for everyone under his control, even to the slaves who were bought with money. We see here missionary spirit of covenant.

Verse 13

"... my covenant shall be in your flesh ..." Philippians 3:3, Romans 8:13 and Galatians 6:17. Abraham must testify that there is nothing in the flesh of value, and he must take the knife to it in sign of the acknowledgment of the covenant.

Verse 14

The one who refused to submit to circumcision was demonstrating his unwillingness to follow God, and must therefore, "be cut off from his people." This meant that he would be exiled from Israel and from any inheritance.

Of course the unsaved will be cut off from salvation. The unsurrendered will be cut off from rewards.

Verse 15

Sarai "my princess." A princess of multitudes. Sarai was almost 90 years old, and so life begins at 90 when you're in the will of God.

Verse 16

This was to be the son of the free woman, the child of grace. Galatians 4:23. The child of fruitfulness. When we are faithful to God, which means we do things His way, we will bear fruit.

Verse 17

His laughter was not laughter of scorn, unbelief,

but rather it was laughter of relief, it was in wonder and happy amazement. <u>God did not rebuke him. Romans 4:18.</u>

Verse 18

What is Ishmael a picture of? The flesh. We see here Abraham's desire for Ishmael. We are to pray for our children, and desire for them to serve God.

Verse 19

God would bless Ishmael, but God first wanted to emphasize again to Abraham that His covenant was with Isaac and Isaac alone and with his seed.

Verse 20

<u>God's ways are not our ways.</u> The flesh can get us into such trouble. The descendants of Ishmael give God's people much trouble. 1. From him came the Arab race. 2. From him came Islam. Trouble for Israel, trouble for Christianity. Ishmael's 12 princes are listed in <u>Genesis 25:12-16</u>.

Verse 21

God repeats the promise, and gives the time. God's mercies promised shall in due time be our exceeding joy.

Verse 22

God having completed the revelation of His covenant <u>"went up."</u>

Verse 23

There is only one way to obey God and that is immediately. The life of faith is the life of obedience to the known will of God.

Verse 24

Abraham had much influence, because he obeyed God. His obedience was speedy, sincere, complete and universal.

CHAPTER 18

Verse 1

Abraham has another visit from God. Jesus appeared with two angels to Abraham. Genesis 32:30, John 1:18.

There is no indication that they had been riding or walking. Abraham looked up and there they were. Abraham somehow sensed that they were very special visitors. His whole manner suggests urgency. He ran and bowed himself down.

"Bowed," Hebrew word "worship." We have here a lesson of reverence in the presence of God.

Verse 3 – 4

Abraham urged the men to rest themselves, while he fetched water to wash their feet and had a meal prepared for them. Abraham addressed the spokesman as "My Lord," (divine name) then addressed himself as "thy servant." He knew this was a providential visit.

Verse 5-8

We see here an exhibition of genuine hospitality. Hebrews 13:2. We must learn to be hospitable. Matthew 25:35.

Abraham stood by them; no doubt he was eager to learn why they had come.

True Christianity teaches us to honor all men.

The Lord put Abraham at ease and sat down to eat.

Verse 9-10

They asked in verse 9, "he said" in verse 10 "the Lord himself did the speaking. Sarah's season for child bearing was to be revived, since her womb had been barren since she was young. This was a miraculous birth. Sarah was past age. One of faiths surest trials is to wait for God's moment. Galatians 4:4.

Verse 11-12

This was a laugh of unbelief. Would you have laughed? Perhaps she did not know yet who these visitors were. Her faith needed to be strengthened, Sarah laughed within herself.

The Lord knew that she laughed, and then He spoke up. Sarah was looking at circumstances while faith must always look to God.

Verse 13-14

This is one of those mountain peak verses of the Bible. The question, "Is any thing too hard for the LORD? ..." The answer, Matthew 19:26. He, who created all things, controls all things.

God specializes in things thought impossible. Unbelief is a doubt of the power of God to perform what He has promised.

Verse 15

Sarah made a flat out denial of her sin. Unbelief

came first then a lie. The Lord rebuked her. Sarah's unbelief did not make the Word of God ineffective. <u>None of His promises would be fulfilled if He stopped because of our unbelief</u>. God is so good to us, He can bring us around. <u>Hebrews 11:11</u>.

Verse 16

The long suffering of the Lord had been <u>exhausted</u> in this case, (<u>Sodom</u>) the time of their judgment was drawing near.

Verse 17

The Lord wanted Abraham to know His intentions toward Sodom and Gomorrah. <u>Abraham needed to know the reasons for the destruction of the cities.</u> <u>He would need to explain it to his children</u>. This event would be a perpetual warning to Israel that, although God is gracious and merciful and long suffering, He is also God of wrath. <u>Jude 7.</u>

Verse 18

Here we have a definite prophecy concerning the Lord Jesus Christ. <u>Galatians 3:8</u>. Here is a clear announcement that the Lord Jesus would come from Abraham.

Faithful Abraham was going to have a tremendous influence.

Notice the seed of Abraham, <u>Genesis 12:12, Galatians 3:29</u>.

Verse 19

God could trust Abraham with the information He was to give. God knew He could trust Abraham to faithfully instruct his descendants. You know God desires righteousness to prevail among men. He is very much interested in all that goes on in our families.

"...the way of the LORD." We have the Word of the Lord, and the way of the Lord. Psalms 138:2, Isaiah 55:9.

His word is important, and His way is important, therefore we must do truth. James 1:22. "But be ye doers of the word, and not hearers only, deceiving your own selves."

Verse 20-21

"I will go down..." In the same way He earlier had come down to Babel. Genesis 11:5. This of course is not that God does not know the full facts without actually going down into the city, He is omniscient. He did this for appearance sake, that men might know directly that God had actually seen the full situation before He acted in judgment.

You know as was true of Abraham, it is vital that believers command their children to keep the way of the Lord.

Verse 22

Abraham the intercessor. "... Abraham stood yet

before the LORD." Abraham's service (hospitality) with his communion with the Lord makes for his growth in the things of God.

Verse 23-33

Here we have the most remarkable example of intercessory prayer in the Bible. Of course Abraham was concerned about Lot and his family, but no doubt was also concerned about others. Abraham knew many of the people there, having saved them years earlier.

Abraham prayed first that the city might be spared if there were 50 righteous people found in it, then 45, then 40, then 30, then 20 and finally 10. Each time God agreed to his request.

Several things to notice here, 1. God does not want to bring judgment, He does respond to the prayer of those who intercede. 2. We see the remarkable influences, which even a tiny minority may have for good. Only 10 people in the corrupt city of Sodom would have been enough to spare it. Let no one think that his/her ministry of prayer is useless. 3. Abraham's prayer was reverent, persistent and definite.

We have here the first example, the first mention of intercessory prayer. The first example of intercessory prayer is in such detail in order to serve as a model.

CHAPTER 19

Verse 1

In chapter 18 Abraham was sitting in the door of his tent, Lot is found sitting at the gate of Sodom.

Abraham had a tent, Lot had a house. Abraham was a pilgrim, Lot was a citizen. Abraham was living for the celestial city, Lot was living for Sodom.

Not only did Lot move into Sodom, but Sodom moved into Lot. Those who sat at the gates of these ancient cities were judges. He got into politics.

Verse 2

Lot was a hospitable man, but his hospitality was in the wrong place.

Verse 3

Here we have the first mention of "leaven." The next time it appears in the Bible is in Exodus 12:15. (Passover)

As we said before Lot was a saved man. Lot was distressed by the wickedness of Sodom. II Peter 2:7-8.

Lot knew it would not be safe for these men to be in the streets all night.

Verse 4

We have a very sickening scene here. We see here the depravity by the wickedness of Sodomites. II

Peter 2:7-8. Here we have case where <u>"...the men of</u>
<u>the city...both old and young...all the people from</u>
<u>every quarter:"</u>

They all surrounded Lot's house with the intention to commit homosexual rape.

Verse 5

The fact that the old men as well as the young
were driven by these lusts, and that rather than
practicing them in secret, they shouted their desires
aloud in the streets shows us how bad the situation
was. It is no wonder God told Abraham that <u>"... the</u>
<u>cry of Sodom and Gomorrah is great, and because</u>
<u>their sin is very grievous;"</u>

What must God think of our current day with,
<u>"gay liberation"</u> and <u>"gay religion?"</u>

Paul gives a burning commentary of this in <u>Ro-</u>
<u>mans 1:26-27</u>. We see the consequences of Lot's
compromise. He did not improve one of Sodom's
citizens.

Verse 6-8

It is hard to understand how Lot could have offered up his two virgin daughters in this way. It is
something to think that his daughters were virgins,
in that awful place. This speaks of some good on
Lot's part. Lot had no influence on these people.

Verse 9

The world has no respect for a compromising Christian. The world expects a Christian to be holy.

Verse 10-11

The angel's intervened. The situation was hopeless, even Lot must have realized there was no remedy but judgment. Lot was in a dangerous place, a worldly Christian is living a dangerous life. Luke 22:55.

Verse 12

If Lot had not known before, he certainly now realized that these men were angels sent from God to judge and destroy.

Lot had nothing to show for all his years of life in Sodom. "A dung heap cannot be perfumed." Lot was one of those Christians saved yet so by fire. I Corinthians 3:15.

Verse 13

How differently God addresses a spiritual Christian from the way He speaks to a carnal Christian. Genesis 18:17. Abraham and Lot received a revelation of the coming destruction of Sodom. To Abraham, walking with God, the Lord quietly revealed His secret.

Verse 14

We have here a deadly example of the deadly results of a father's compromise with the world. The Bible forbids mixed marriages. If Lot had not gone to Sodom, his daughters would not have Sodomite husbands. There can be no fellowship between the light of a Christian life and the darkness of an unbeliever's life. II Corinthians 6:14. Nehemiah tells the terrible story of the children of Ashdod and Ismel who spoke half in one language and half in the other. Nehemiah 13:23-25.

Verse 15

It is a sad commentary when Christians have to be pushed into the things, which are for their own good.

Here we have a "backslider." The true meaning of the word is illustrated by Lots conduct. Notice in verse 16 "...he lingered..." Turn to Hosea 4:16. Any stockman who has loaded heifers will understand this. Heifers are like backsliding Christians, they must be pushed.

Verse 16

"...he lingered..." How could Lot have any affection for a place where the people were so filthy, so depraved? How could a just man linger in a city where he had almost sacrificed the honor of his daughters? This is an amazing picture of the lust of the flesh against the Spirit. Galatians 5:17, I Peter 2:11.

"...the LORD being merciful unto him..." It was the Lord's mercy that Lot was <u>pushed</u> and <u>pulled</u> out by the angels. "*It is of* the LORD'S mercies that we are not consumed..." And the reason is "<u>...his compassions fail not."</u> <u>Lamentations 3:22-23</u>.

Verse 17

The angels had to use drastic measures and dramatic language. The time of God's vengeance was at hand. There was no safety now except in flight. The message against sin is the same today. <u>Jude 7</u>.

Even in sight of Sodom, God had provided a mountain of refuge. <u>God has provided the mountain of Calvary</u>. If we have escaped to the Lord Jesus Christ, no judgment can fall upon us, justice has been satisfied forever. <u>Proverbs 18:10</u>.

No one is safe if they linger outside of Jesus.

"<u>...look not behind thee...</u>" <u>Philippians 3:13-14</u>. We must learn to obey God.

Verse 18

It seems incredible that Lot would argue with his rescuers, but drowning men sometimes fight those who seek to keep their heads above water. Lot's prayer was, <u>"not thy will but mine be done."</u> He is determined to have his own way.

Verse 19

The contrast is maintained to the end. When

Abraham prayed to the Lord, he saw himself as dust and ashes. Lot on the other hand took every step to get his own way.

Verse 20

The little sin is most dangerous, for it always leads to greater sins. The Lord had commanded that Lot escape to the mountain for safety, Lot lingers, this believer wanted his own way and bad. This shows us how bad our old nature really is.

God records the whimpering of Lot to show us what we are in ourselves. Remember, Song of Solomon 2:15, I Corinthians 5:6. Moses chose affliction rather Than pleasures. Hebrews 11:25-26. Moses realizes that God would do more for him than he could do for himself. Lot never learned that. Leave the choice with God.

Verse 21

We have here a mystery. Was God kind to Lot or was Lot delivered over to his own desires? The disastrous results of Lot's choice prove it was not God's choice for him. Be careful what you ask for. Psalms 106:7-15.

Verse 22

What an example of the patience of God toward the wicked because of the presence of the saved among them. The world hates the believers and yet the Lord speaks of them as <u>"the light of the world, the salt of the earth."</u> Without the presence of the believers the world would be in darkness and would be rottenness.

Verse 23-24

Judgment has its source in God. <u>Judgment is decided by God, executed by God. God runs hell, God manages the lake of fire.</u> When the devil reaches the lake of fire he will be its number one prisoner, <u>not the jailer.</u>

We see the certainty of judgment upon every abomination. <u>Numbers 32:23, Ecclesiastes 12:14</u>.

Verse 25

What God did to these ancient cities, He will do again. <u>Luke 17:28-30</u>. <u>"The day"</u> <u>Hebrews 10:25</u>.

Verse 26

<u>Her heart was in Sodom</u>, even though they were leaving. We cannot sin and not be affected. Jesus said the words that go forth as a trumpet, <u>"Remember Lot's wife." Luke 17:32</u>. God struck her dead for looking back, she becomes a monument to all future generations that God's demands are to turn whole heartedly away from the world.

She was as salt with no savor, worthless, her physical body in its judgment warns against carnal love, and its association. <u>I John 2:15</u>.

Verse 27

Abraham had gone home, <u>18:33</u>. He awakes and goes back to the place of <u>sweet communion</u>, and of <u>intercessory prayer.</u>

Verse 28

There is no record that Abraham ever saw Lot again. What he had been commanded to do 40 years before was finally accomplished. <u>12:1</u>. God's <u>people just keep going</u>.

There must be <u>complete obedience</u> to God and a <u>complete separation</u> before we can <u>be fruitful</u> for <u>God in His way</u>.

Verse 29

We see here the importance of Intercessory prayer.

Verse 30

One of the most dangerous things that a Christian can do is to move without the leading of the Holy Spirit. Lot had been running his own life. He pitched his tent toward Sodom; he moved into it, he sat at the gate. When God pushed him out he pleaded to move into Zoar. He is now fretful, when a man is out of the will of God; he is haunted by his own imagination. Lot loved only himself. No matter where he goes he must take himself along, and so his problem is ever with him.

"…in a cave…" Abraham lived in a tent beside an alter. Lot chose a cave, which was a place of death in those days, because a cave was often the symbol of the tomb. Lot was like the women in I Timothy 5:6.

Lot is lonely, but he was eating the fruit of his own doing. He chose Sodom and lost his wife and family. God was gracious to rescue his two daughters, but they brought the ways of Sodom with them. Lot had put himself ahead of God and his family.

Verse 31

If Lot would have gone God's way, he would have lived in peace as Abraham. Lot did not and as a result he wrecked his life and his families.

Verse 32

Lot had offered up his daughters to the filthy men of Sodom and now that lustful sin has surfaced in his daughters. The Bible says, "Honor thy father and thy mother." Many children have made shipwreck of their lives because they would not submit to their parents. There can be no true blessing from God for anybody who fails to give respect to parents.

Verse 33

Drink can blind, can cause loss of self control. And causes acts of sin according to the heart. When you get saved God gives you anew heart.

Verse 34

The older influence the younger. We must be examples for Christ. Lot's daughter influenced the younger to commit sin. Both were guilty but the older sister was much guiltier.

Verse 36

God teaches us here that believers who get out of the will of God and produce fruit by their own efforts must be judged by God.

Verse 37-38

James 1:13-16. Lots life perfectly illustrates this truth. Hundreds of years afterward the children of Moab and Ammon opposed Israel from Egypt to Canaan.

The Fruit of the flesh opposes the fruit of the spirit.

CHAPTER 20

Verse 1

Gerar the capital city at that time of the land of the <u>Philistines</u>. It is hard to understand how they could have forgotten the rebuke of this course of action from before down in Egypt. A Christian can move from victory to sin and defeat. Abraham had been guilty of this same sin before and had been reproved for it. It is possible that a good man not only falls into sin, but into the same sin. Not only that Sarah was with child no doubt and should have been protected.

Verse 2

Sarah was 90 years old and was still physically attractive. She had been physically rejuvenated in order to conceive, bear and nurse Isaac.

The man of faith has no right to deceive the world around him. This is a lie, <u>half truth is a lie</u>. There is no good in man, no matter how far he may have advanced with the Lord. Anything that is good in any man is that which comes from the Lord, and all that is wrong comes from man. Abraham had the nature of Adam, and so do we.

Satan here was seeking to pollute the womb of Sarah. <u>Satan makes war with God.</u>

Verse 3

<u>"But God..."</u> Regardless of their mistake, God would not allow His promise to Abraham and Sarah be broken. God appears to Abimelech in a dream. We see here what God thinks of a man taking another mans wife. We see here what God thinks of marriage.

Verse 4

Abimelech was a Gentile King and knew not God as Jehovah but as God the Creator. The Philistine Nation was not a righteous nation. If God spared Gerar it was not because of anything good in them, it was purely God's Grace.

Verse 5

Abimelech pleads ignorance. Oh how Abraham was out of the will of God. A Christian out of the will of God can spread <u>spiritual infection</u> that will have dire consequences. It is regrettable that by human standards many unsaved people are more honorable than saved people. The unsaved stand in another land and look across into our land and see truths that belong not to them for they have not the nature that we have by grace. So Christian guard and keep your testimony before God and the world.

Verse 6

There is nothing hid from God. Abimelech acted honorably by the <u>restraining power of God</u>, not through his nature. Abimelech already has a wife, verse 17. He sent for Sarah to satisfy his fleshly desires. God was protecting the line of the seed of the woman. <u>3:15</u>. God mentioned here that sin is against Him.

Verse 7

<u>First mention of prophet</u>. Abraham is called a prophet here, not one that predicts the future, <u>but</u> a man representing God. God always takes care of those who are his. Abraham would pray for Abimelech. Abraham no matter how feeble was <u>God's man.</u> Abraham would pray and Abimelech would be spared because of Abraham. <u>You know people can be spared if we will care enough to pray</u>.

Verse 8

The smell of Sodom's sulfur was now a memory, but what a memory. Oh how God strikes terror upon the nations. <u>Judgment is real</u>, when judgment is seen in others someone needs to take wise notice.

Verse 9

Once again Abraham experiences a stinging rebuke from a heathen. <u>Oh how God used Abimelech's rebuke</u>. Abraham and Sarah's experience in Egypt now was brought to memory, along with its bitterness and shame. This is a shameful moment for the old man. It would have been bad enough to be rebuked by another believer, but to be rebuked by a heathen.

Verse 10-11

Abraham gave his excuse; he should have said "forgive me." We will get into trouble every time when we rely on our own thinking instead of the Word of God. Psalms 94:11. I read where an old Scotch lady said "I have learned that in the long run the Almighty is correct." Psalms 119:11. There is never any excuse for sin. Abraham had no right to give his excuse to Abimelech; he was dead wrong and should have said so.

"...I thought, Surely the fear of God *is* not in this place..." but it was, verse 8. Abimelech was still shaking in his boots. Oh how we need to trust the Lord.

Verse 12

This half lie is not right. Although Sarah was Abraham's half-sister the fact remained she was his wife. We all need to be careful, we all as Christians have the old nature. I Corinthians 10:12.

Verse 13

"Wander," this word means, "As animals go astray," of a drunken man reeling to and fro, staggering. One of the terrible things of sin is to blame God. Adam said to God, "The woman thou gavest me..." And so we see here Abraham showing his traits of his father Adam. This can happen to Christians. Be careful. Oh how we must be careful. Luke 16:8. Stay in the "Word," and "Pray." Luke 18:1.

"I said unto her..." Abraham himself had originated this deception of sin Romans 7:18, 24 & 8:2.

"...This *is* thy kindness which thou shalt shew unto me..." A lie is never a kindness. Nothing gained by sin is worth the price paid for it. "...the deceitfulness of sin." Hebrews 3:12-13.

Our own selfish interest causes us to break fellowship with God. Let's see what God thinks of self interest. Luke 12:20-21.

Verse 14
The Philistine King is now heaping coals of fire upon the head of Abraham. Abraham should have given Abimelech a large gift, but the pagan king, victim of deception, gives a present to Abraham.

It is sad when a lost man rebukes a believer. Instead of being a blessing to others he becomes a temptation.

In any event Abimelech did restore Sarah to Abraham; again we are reminded of God's protective hand upon His own.

Verse 15

Abraham refused to take a spoil from the four king confederation when he rescued Lot. He now accepts probably as to not further offend Alimelech.

Verse 16

Sarah was reproved. It is as if Alimelech is saying to Sarah, "Listen Abraham is your husband, and he is God's prophet, you have no need to fear." I do not believe there were ever more stinging words from Jesus lips to His disciples than, "...O ye of little faith..."

Verse 17

Here we see the power of the Abrahamic Covenant shine through. The sovereign grace of God shines out with brilliance; Work's has nothing to do with salvation. If it did, Abraham would have failed before now, Abraham failed but he keeps on going.

Verse 18

The covenant was made with Abraham and touched his wife Sarah.

Pray not to be a stumbling block. God closed their wombs; God goes to great lengths to fulfill His Word.

CHAPTER 21

1. The birth of Isaac in verses 1 thru 8.
2. The departure of Ishmael in verses 9 thru 13.
3. The kindness of God in verses 14 thru 21.
4. Abraham and Abimelech verses 22 thru 34.

Finally after twenty-five years in the land of Canaan waiting for the fulfillment of God's promise, Abraham's faith was rewarded. Paul gives us a commentary of this great event. Romans 4:17-22.

Abraham is a type of all who are, "...justified by faith." Paul stresses that Abraham was justified by faith not by circumcision in Romans 4:9-12. And Paul tells us that Abraham was justified by faith not the law. Galatians 3:16-18. Salvation depends not on ritual or law, but by Grace, received through faith.

Verse 1

"As he had said...as he had spoken." Look at Genesis 18:9-14. This first verse in Genesis 21 emphasizes that God keeps His Word. God's promise was fulfilled according to His schedule not man's. Verse 2, "...at the set time..." Galatians 4:4.

God is a God of His word. If he were not, the universe would fall apart.

Verse 2

Like Abraham, we often become impatient waiting for God to work, <u>but</u> like Abraham we should learn <u>to be strong in faith</u> giving glory to God, and be <u>fully persuaded</u> that what God promises, <u>He is able to perform</u>.

The first mention of Sarah is in <u>Genesis 11:30</u>, we read she was barren, and then she laughed when she heard she would have a baby in a year. <u>Genesis 18:12-14.</u> She was 90 years old and from human stand point had every right to laugh. <u>But</u> faith looks at things from God's stand point. <u>Hebrews 11:11.</u>

God's set time, not our set time is the <u>best time.</u> What God says <u>certainly comes to pass!</u>

Verse 3

Isaac – "<u>Laughter</u>," an appropriate name. Every time His name was mentioned there was laughter. <u>Abraham laughed in amazement, in joy</u>. <u>Genesis 17:17</u>. Sarah laughed in doubt in <u>Genesis 18:12</u>. Great joy when He was born for all the earth, verse 6.

Verse 4-5

When Isaac was 8 days old, Abraham circumcised him, as God commanded in <u>17:12</u>. This son was loved very much. His mother and father taught him the ways of righteousness, <u>18:19.</u> He was an obedient son. Abraham was 100 years old at Isaac's birth.

Verse 6

Whatever God does He does well. It is as if Sarah was singing, Psalms 126:2-3. This baby filled her with joy. God caused her to rejoice and gave her a heart to rejoice. God is the source of our joy. He is not the source of the fool's joy.

Verse 7

Sarah was filled with wonder. What had happened was near impossible. Oh how God favors His children. His Son was sent to die for us; such great sins all pardoned praise the Lord!

Verse 8

It is a great occasion when a baby grows and learns to eat meat. This pictures the child of God who need's to grow from the milk of the Word to the meat of the Word. Hebrews 5:12-14.

Verse 9

Genesis 21 should be carefully compared with Galatians 4. Genesis 21 provides historical facts while Galatians 4 provides the spiritual significance.

There is no fellowship, no communion between Ishmael and Isaac. One is the son of a slave, the other the son of a free woman. One is of the flesh; one is of God's grace. The flesh persecutes the spirit. Galatians 4:29.

Verse 10

Sin always has a chain reaction. Sarah's sin is expanding, and is cruel. Hagar had no choice when her baby was given to Abraham. She bore the child at Sarah's suggestion. Sarah could not tolerate what she was seeing now between the two boys. <u>It is impossible to have joy in any way but God's way.</u>

The seed of Hagar rises against the seed of Sarah. <u>Grace and law cannot mix</u>. The law cannot dwell in the house of faith.

Verse 11

Sarah's attitude was a source of grief to Abraham. Sin hurts. We can understand Abraham's love to his first born son. Abraham enjoyed Ishmael for years. And so Abraham wanted to hang on to the flesh but it had to go. You know we got our flesh nature before we got our new nature. <u>The flesh has to be reckoned dead.</u> <u>Romans 6:6, 11-13.</u>

Verse 12

There are times when we need to listen to our wives. <u>Amen.</u> <u>Sarah's attitude was in accord with God's will</u>. We must do the will of God at all cost; we must disregard our feelings, knowing that the true blessing will come as we are <u>surrendered to God</u>. The stories of Cain and Abel, Isaac and Ishmael, Jacob and Esau illustrate to us the entire human race. <u>Malachi 1:2-3.</u> <u>This simply means that God hates</u>

the flesh. Genesis 4:3-4.

When Abraham was brought low God is there to comfort to sustain him in his sorrow.

Verse 13

Notice <u>Genesis 17:18</u>. Abraham's desire for Ishmael. God promised Abraham that Ishmael also would become a great nation. <u>Romans 11:33.</u>

And so for hundreds of years The Arab's have been in the land of Israel and have been an <u>irritation to the Jews</u>.

Verse 14-15

<u>God will not allow grace to be mocked by the law.</u> <u>Galatians 4:29-31</u>. This was no doubt hard for Abraham, but he obeyed the Lord. Isaac was the son of promise. Nevertheless <u>God assured Abraham that He would take care of Ishmael</u> for he was to become a great nation. <u>Matthew 5:45</u>. God is good to all!

Verse 16

We see total lack of faith on Hagar's part, because God told her that He would multiply her descendants exceedingly. <u>Genesis 16:10</u>. She should have believed the promise, but she represents the law, which cannot comprehend grace through faith. <u>Romans 4:19-20.</u> <u>Abraham looked at death and saw life, Hagar looked at her living son and saw death.</u> Oh what a difference faith makes.

Verse 17-18

To complain against the providences of God is the sin of unbelief. It is so with the godly and ungodly. God made a promise and to whine when it gets difficult is to doubt God's Word. To suggest that the lad would die is to deny the Word of God. Genesis 16:10.

Verse 19

What a difference between a believer and an unbeliever. Isaac lived his life near wells, Ishmael lived in the desert. Isaiah 12:3, John 4:14, Revelation 22:17.

Verse 20

The child of Grace has the sword as his weapon. Ishmael the child of bondage was one with Nimrod and Esau, the archers. Genesis 49:22-23. Satan has fiery darts, he hates grace and shoots at grace. Thank God we as the children of grace do not need to be afraid. Psalms 91:5.

Verse 21

Ishmael obtained a wife from his mother's people. We read of the son's of Ishmael in Genesis 25:13-15. The great promise of God had begun.

Verse 22

"...God *is* with thee in all that thou doest:" We now have recorded an incident between Abraham

and Abimelech. The same king that Abraham en-
countered in <u>Gerar.</u> Abimelech was aware of God's
blessing on Abraham. It is impossible for a believer
to walk with God without the world noticing the
power of God. <u>Acts 4:13.</u>

Verse 23

Abimelech with these words, "<u>... swear unto
me here by God that thou wilt not deal falsely with
me...</u>" rebuked Abraham.

Isaac had been born to Abraham and Sarah who
were past age, a true miracle of God. This fact along
with God's conversation with Abimelech. This made
Abimelech afraid of Abraham. He thought it best to
be at peace with this man of God.

Verse 24

Abraham was willing to make this covenant. The
believer is to be a man or woman of peace where no
compromise is involved. <u>Colossians 4:5, I Thessalonians 4:12, I Timothy 3:7.</u>

God wants us His children to live in this world
in such a way that we will have His favor and grace
upon our lives. So the world will see that we are the
objects of His love and care. Abraham's willingness
here showed he was a man of peace. <u>Matthew 5:9,
Proverbs 12:20, Romans 14:19.</u> We must win the
lost with our godly lives.

Verse 25-26

Abraham had dug a well. Some of Abimelech's servants had raided the area and captured the well from Abraham's servants. Abimelech did not know about it and quickly returned the well.

The believer may make a covenant with an unbeliever but must protest any attempt to touch his well. Water is a symbol of the Word of God. We are not to live by bread alone but by every word that proceeds out of the mouth of God. Deuteronomy 8:3, Matthew 4:4. The world will attack our water supply (the Word of God), We cannot walk with those who would contaminate our water supply.

Verse 27

Abraham did not compromise the well but was a wise peaceful man. He gave a gift to Abimelech. II Timothy 2:24-25.

Abraham gave 7 ewe lambs. Seven the number of completeness, thus sealing the covenant. Which shows Abraham's permanent right to the well. Beersheba – "the well of the seven," "the well of the oath."

Verse 32-34

"Jehovah, El-Olam" – "Jehovah is the eternal God."

CHAPTER 22

Where in all the Bible is there a chapter like <u>Genesis 22</u>. <u>Psalms 22</u> shows us what Calvary meant to the Son. <u>Genesis 22</u> shows us what Calvary meant to the Father.

All that Mt. Moriah meant to Abraham, the agony and heartache and pain, that a thousand fold, ten-thousand fold, is what Calvary meant to God.

<u>The trial of Abraham's faith.</u> This is the first time human sacrifice is even suggested. <u>God is not in human sacrifice</u>.

A life must be given up in order for God to save sinners.

This chapter is a <u>trial</u>, a <u>test</u> of Abraham's <u>faith and obedience</u> and also a <u>picture of Calvary</u>. No man was worthy to die for man, but the Lord Jesus Christ.

Verse 1

The word <u>"tempt"</u> – <u>"to prove,"</u> God tempts no man. <u>"Prove,"</u> Satan tempts us that he may bring out the evil that is in our hearts. God <u>tries</u> or <u>tests</u> us that He may bring out all the good.

<u>James 1:13</u>, "here I am." We see the obedience of Abraham. Abraham was in the practice of hearing and obeying God.

We see two great principals in Abraham's life. <u>1.</u>

Faith. <u>2.</u> Obedience. In chapter 22 we see a supreme illustration of <u>"surrender."</u> In chapter 12 Abraham left home and country. In chapter 13 Abraham gave up land to Lot. In chapter 14 Abraham turned down the offer of The King of Sodom. In chapter 21 Abraham gave up Ishmael. In Chapter 22 Abraham surrendered Isaac.

Verse 2

<u>"...thine only *son*..."</u> Did not Isaac have a brother? Ishmael. God does not recognize the flesh. No natural man will enter heaven; no man of the flesh will be in heaven. God had no intention that Abraham would sacrifice his son. Oh how this verse played the heart strings of Abraham's heart. <u>"...whom thou lovest..."</u>

<u>"...the land of Moriah..."</u> Jesus died on this same mountain.

Verse 3

<u>"...rose up early in the morning..."</u> Abraham believed God and was therefore <u>ready to obey.</u> Delayed obedience is <u>disobedience.</u>

Abraham's response was 1. <u>Swift</u> – "rose up early in the morning." <u>Psalms 119:60.</u> 2. <u>Unquestioning</u> – He had already obeyed when he knew not where. <u>Hebrews 11:8</u>; he now obeys when he knew not why.

No matter how much faith Abraham had, the test

was no less severe. He went forth to the test, trusting God; he went forward with an <u>aching heart.</u>

Notice what David said in <u>Psalms 119:60.</u> Abraham takes his son and the Word.

Verse 4

<u>The third day</u>. Illustration of the Resurrection. <u>Hebrews 11:17-19.</u> Abraham trusted the Lord. Abraham seen past the immediate and saw the Lord Jesus Christ. <u>John 8:56.</u>

The one <u>"place"</u> foreshadowed the other. <u>Luke 23:33.</u>

Verse 5

<u>"Worship"</u> – <u>Submission to God's will is worship.</u> Worship, to bow down. Abraham told the young men to stay. <u>Faith must always go alone with God.</u> "…and come again to you…" Again we see Abraham believed God. Abraham and Isaac went (Father and Son).

<u>"God and the Son of God,"</u> man had nothing to do with the cross. <u>Mark 14:33-36.</u> Jesus and the Father.

Verse 6

<u>Jesus Christ carried His cross.</u> The fire speaks of judgment. And so the lessons are, 1. <u>Isaac</u> – Type of Christ, "obedient unto death." 2. <u>Abraham</u> – Type of the Father. 3. <u>The Ram</u> – Type of substitution. 4.

The Resurrection.

Verse 7

Isaac was fully aware that blood would have to be shed. Isaac's question sunk into Abraham's heart. Where is our heart when we come to worship God? Oh how it needs to be tender and close to God.

Verse 8

Faithful Abraham, oh what faith this man had. He walked steadfastly to his trial. God did not force the Son of God to go to the cross. John 10:17-18. It was the Father's will and the Son willing obeyed. We see here again that Abraham believed in the resurrection. "...God will provide himself a lamb..." John 1:29.

Verse 9

Abraham's heart was heavy, but he went on in obedience. We see here a picture of a glorious truth in that Isaac was a willing sacrifice. Isaac had a personal faith that was joined to that of Abraham. God tested Abraham and Abraham passed the test. Let us pray that we will pass the test.

Verse 10

With consent Isaac submits and allows Abraham his father, his senior by 100 years, to bind him upon the altar. We see they both together obeyed, yielded, cooperating even as the Heavenly Father and the Lord Jesus Christ did at Calvary. They both believed that out of this God would bring forth resurrection life.

Verse 11

God has sufficiently tested the faith of His servant. Abraham had demonstrated that he believed God, loved God and trusted God.

"Here *am* I..." this is the second time Abraham says "Here *am* I..." He who is obedient to God's command when it is grievous will enjoy the command that brings joy. The biggest percentage of knowing the will of God is in our willingness to do His bidding as Abraham did.

Verse 12

The angel of the Lord commended Abraham because, "...thou hast not withheld thy son, thine only son from me." It's evident that this angel of the Lord is none other than the Lord himself.

God knew what the outcome would be all along, but now Abraham knows. God shares His knowledge with us. This testing of Abraham would stand for generations to come as an example of God's faithfulness.

Best evidence of our fearing God is our being willing to serve and honor Him with that, which is dearest to us.

Verse 13

Abraham said in verse 8, "...God will provide Himself a lamb..." God did exactly that except that it was a ram instead of a lamb. The complete fulfillment was the Lamb of God. The ram was offered up on the alter as a burnt offering in substitution for Isaac, thus teaching the substitutionary sacrifice of Jesus Christ. The Temple, the place of sacrifice was built upon Mt. Moriah. II Chronicles 3:1.

Verse 14

"Jehovah – Jireh" The Lord will provide. As Abraham said in verse 8 "...God will provide..." The Lord will intervene for His people in the hour of their necessity.

It is said to this day, God is the same at all times for all His people. The fountainhead of His provision is the cross of the Lord Jesus Christ.

"...In the mount of the LORD it shall be seen." The Mount of the Lord is Calvary. If we go to the Mount of the Lord we shall be blessed, nothing can stop the blessing that flows from Calvary.

Verse 15

To the one who has manifested triumphant faith will come instruction, blessings and the glories of God. Heaven pronounces blessings upon the child of faith. Remember even in your sorest trial just keep going and trusting in Christ. We are taught here that the Lord will intervene for us in our hour of need. <u>Psalms 34:4, 7, 17, 19.</u>

This action of Abraham caused God to bear a wonderful testimony on his behalf. God will not require you to offer up an only son, <u>but</u> notice what He does require. <u>Luke 14:26.</u> That means any of these as in comparison with Jesus.

Verse 16

Abraham's actions caused God to speak from heaven and renew His promise to Abraham. <u>Hebrews 6:13-18.</u> We being the heirs of promise, God is comforting us here. His promise is the anchor of our soul. God is pleased to make mention of Abraham's obedience.

Verse 17

The key to this promise is not Abraham but our Lord Jesus Christ. <u>Galatians 3:16.</u>

"...I will multiply thy seed as the stars of the heaven, and as the sand which *is* upon the sea shore..." The number is more than we can comprehend. The church, the body of Christ will be with Him in glory.

"...and thy seed shall possess the gate of his enemies;" <u>By Jesus death upon the cross and His resurrection,</u> He laid the foundation for sin to be abolished. He abolished death forever. <u>II Timothy 1:10.</u> As the risen Lord He said in <u>Revelation 1:18.</u>

On the cross He spoiled the powers of Satan. <u>Colossians 2:15.</u>

Verse 18

<u>Galatians 3:16.</u> First mention of the word, <u>"obey."</u> Obedience belongs to God first of all, and that <u>obedience to God</u> results in <u>rich blessings</u>. We show by our obedience that we believe He is good, wise and loving. Amen!

Verse 19

Abraham told the young men that he and Isaac would return in verse 5. And now they both come down the hill together. What a blessed sight. Oh what joy there was in all their hearts. Beersheba is where Abraham made his home.

Verse 20-24

Family of Nahor, Abraham's brother. Rebekah came from this family, as we will see in <u>Genesis 24.</u>

CHAPTER 23

Verse 1-2

The tie between Abraham and Sarah was very sweet and strong. We do not know how long the time between the offering up of Isaac and the death of Sarah was. Isaac was 37 years old when his mother died.

We are to look at Sarah as an example. Isaiah 51:1-2, I Peter 3:4-7. Sarah is the only woman in the Bible whose age at the time of death was given. She is one of the outstanding women of the Bible.

Evidentially Abraham was not present at the time of her death. Verse 2, "...Abraham came to mourn for Sarah, and to weep for her." This suggests that her death was quick, for if she would have had a terminal illness, Abraham would have been home. He loved her dearly.

Thank God He is ever with us. Isaiah 63:9, It is note worthy that the first actual possession of Abraham in his so journey was a grave.

Not only did Abraham love Sarah, but Isaac loved her very much too. Genesis 24:67.

Sarah was the first in the patriarchal family line to die in the land of Canaan.

Verse 3

Again the only purchase of property Abraham

made in the land of Canaan was for a grave, though he had many possessions, he himself had no certain dwelling place. <u>Hebrews 11:9.</u>

We must go on and live, "Lord, we thank Thee for the strength to live life," we must go on.

Verse 4

We must own a bit of dust to receive our dust. The death of our loved ones reminds us that we are not at home in this world.

Verse 5-6

A holy life affects the minds of men. At first it may offend, but in the long haul they are forced to acknowledge. The children of Heth did not know Abraham's God, but they knew Abraham and were forced to glorify his God. <u>Matthew 5:16.</u>

Verse 7

Twice, verses 7 and 12 His manner of dealing with people of the world is an example for believers today. <u>An attitude of superiority is inappropriate.</u>

Abraham showed great courtesy. <u>I Peter 3:8.</u> Take a look at <u>Philippians 2:3.</u>

We are to have good manners.

Verse 8-15

Ephron and Abraham transacted their business openly before all.

Ephron was going to give the field to Abraham.

Abraham insisted on buying it. <u>Honesty and honor is best.</u>

Verse 16

Abraham weighed out the silver. In those days prices were paid in terms of weights. Abraham was very rich.

Verse 17

This land was ideal, for Abraham he could see her burying place from where he lived.

Abraham was buying the field not only to bury Sarah but also to express his confidence in God's promise. He was waiting for the great resurrection day.

And so in chapter 23 our dealings with men of this world, and the blessed hope that we have in the resurrection of Jesus Christ, <u>is seen.</u>

<u>Faith</u> makes a man independent of the world. <u>Faith</u> will teach him to walk honestly toward them. <u>I Thessalonians 4:12, II Corinthians 8:21.</u>

CHAPTER 24

Genesis 24 is the longest chapter in the Book of Genesis. Entire books have been written about this chapter.

Isaac is a type of Christ, and there are a lot of parallels between the story of Isaac's search for a bride, through the Father's trusted servant, and the sending forth of the Holy Spirit to take out the Gentiles, a people for His name. Acts 15:14. A bride for Christ, II Corinthians 11:2. You will notice that Abraham's servant goes unnamed in this story. The Holy Spirit never speaks of Himself. John 16:13-14, 14:26.

Of greater importance than symbolism is the fact that the bride selected for Isaac had to be chosen with particular care since she would be the mother of the multitude of nations, which God had promised would come through Abraham's seed, through which the promised Saviour would come. Though this marriage is very important, so is the institution of marriage very important to God. It would be well for all young people and their parents to study this carefully. Abraham pictures the Father, Isaac the Son, unnamed servant the Holy Spirit and Rebekah the Church.

Verse 1

No matter how great our faith, we must all come to the grave. Abraham was 140 years old. <u>We are born and will die</u>. Let husbands, wives, children and all remember this, <u>enjoy one another, there is not much time</u>.

"...the LORD had blessed Abraham in all things." Abraham had been slow to obey, but God had blessed him in all things. He did not separate from his kindred for years, but God blessed him in all things. He went into Egypt, but God blessed him in all things. He had Sarah lie and was on the point of seeing her dishonored, but God blessed him in all things. He lapsed from faith and dishonored God in the land of Abimelech, but God blessed Abraham in all things. <u>God's dealings are in grace</u>, and totally unrelated to any worth in the man to whom the promises are made. <u>It is all of grace</u>.

Verse 2

This was a most <u>solemn oath</u>, and was clearly related to God's promise in connection to the promised land, and seed. We see here the <u>sacredness of life.</u> It was very important to Abraham, his request to his servant. <u>Abraham considered the choice of a bride for Isaac as important as life itself.</u>

Verse 3

It was very, very, very important that Isaac and

his wife be completely united in <u>their faith</u>, <u>in their</u> <u>covenant with God</u>, in order to properly instruct <u>their children in the faith</u>. To find the right wife for Isaac, Abraham must search among his own people. Abraham knew there must be such a girl somewhere, because he trusted God to provide the promised seed through Isaac. We read of Rebekah in <u>Genesis 22:20, 23.</u>

"...<u>the God of heaven</u>..." The God of glory appeared to Abraham in Ur. <u>Acts 7:2.</u> Abraham impresses upon his servant <u>Eliezer</u> that his God is the <u>God of glory</u>. "...<u>and the God of the earth</u>..." God is the God of the earth because He is the God of heaven. This earth we live on is but a speck of dust in comparison to the universe. <u>But the Lord picked</u> <u>it out to be the stage on which the drama of cre-</u> <u>ation, judgment, redemption, and victory should be</u> <u>played.</u> <u>Here</u> Lucifer sinned, <u>here</u> was the first judgment, <u>here</u> Adam fell and above all <u>here</u> Jesus Christ lived and died, and rose again. <u>John 17:4.</u>

Verse 4-9

Abraham was too old to make the long trip. Abraham was very strong that Isaac not go. (Verse 6-8). The heir of God's promise should <u>stay in the</u> <u>Promised Land.</u> Isaac never left the land of Canaan. <u>Genesis 26:2-3.</u> If Isaac had gone in search of a bride, there might have been too great a temptation for him to stay with her among her own people. <u>She must be willing to come to him.</u> <u>We must come to Christ by faith.</u> He sends for us through the Holy Spirit. <u>Jesus is the bridegroom, we are the bride.</u>

Verse 8

We make the choice to come to Christ or not to come to Him. The Holy Spirit does His work.

Verse 9

The precious Holy Spirit does His work very well. He is faithful. <u>John 16:7-11.</u> We find that Eliezer did well; he did just as he was commanded.

Verse 10

The servant sets out on his journey. Taking all of the provisions needed. The long journey was difficult no doubt, but was not mentioned by God. In this story Isaac and Rebekah are emphasized rather than the servant. <u>John 16:13-14, 14:26.</u>

In verse 11 Eliezer arrives early in the evening after a long journey, and now <u>prays for wisdom.</u> <u>Oh how wise.</u>

Verse 11

The <u>caravan</u> stopped at the edge of the city by the well. Abraham's servant knew that the woman of the place would come out to the wells to draw water for their households in the early evening, and so this seemed to be the best place to meet them.

Verse 12-14

While the party was waiting and resting Abraham's servant did not rest but prayed. They made it this far safely, but how was he to know which girl he should choose for his master? He knew some of the qualities she must have. <u>She must be from Abraham's people; she must be godly, and virtuous.</u> But many girls could be like this. The servant might have also thought, she should be <u>strong</u> and <u>healthy</u> and <u>pretty</u>. She should be <u>gracious</u> and <u>considerate</u>, <u>compassionate</u> and <u>sensitive.</u> How could Abraham's servant determine which of the girls that would be coming soon would have these qualities? <u>He didn't have much time.</u> He would approach and ask for a drink of water. Most any girl would have common courtesy and give him a drink. But if she would of her <u>own initiative</u> offer to <u>go the second mile</u>, that would be a good sign. It was hard work to give water to ten thirsty camels, to do this without grumbling would be a good sign that she was the one.

Abraham's servant made a specific request. He had been led of the Lord to that point, and it was appropriate for him to make this request. This is a <u>good example of specific believing prayer.</u> He needed definite guidance, not general direction. Therefore he prayed specifically. Each day trust the Lord for firmness and decision in all that you have to do. <u>"Lord, keep us in Thy calm activity."</u>

Verse 15

Isaiah 65:24, Praise God! We need to be walking close to God. Believe not only in the long range will of God, but also in the short range will of God. Trusting God moment by moment. "Lord may we not be satisfied with anything less than being drenched with Thy will." She, Rebekah was the first one out. This was hard work, and she was the first one out, which speaks well of her character.

Verse 16

God does talk about physical beauty, Acts 7:20, Hebrews 11:23. We read of this fairness in those who lack beauty in the inward parts. I Samual16:6-7. God desires truth in the inward parts. A picture here of the church being fit for the altogether Lovely One. Ephesians 5:27.

Verse 17

The servant's prayer in verse 14 now starts to unfold. This girl who would give a stranger a drink of water would certainly have a good disposition. Matthew 10:42. We can only imagine the thrill of the servant when God immediately sent this girl who had it all.

Verse 18

Christians are to be courteous. I Peter 3:8. We are to prefer others before ourselves. Romans 12:10.

True courtesy will arise from esteeming others better than ourselves. <u>Philippians 2:3.</u> We honor the
Lord by being courteous.

Verse 19

One camel would drink more than <u>20 gallons.</u>
This was hard work for Rebekah. She was not afraid
of work. Let the church not be afraid of hard work
for God.

Verse 20

Rebekah worked hard and was blessed. <u>Romans
12:11.</u> "Lord make us diligent."

Verse 21

The servant did not know who she was yet, although he watched her and marveled, he <u>"held his
peace."</u> He <u>"wondering"</u> at the way God was answer-
ing his prayer.

Verse 22

God is very generous; we can never out give
God.

Verse 23

The servant now asks the all important question.
<u>"Whose daughter art thou?</u>

Verse 24

She was the granddaughter of Abraham's brother.

Verse 25-26

The servant stopped and had to bow down and worship the Lord. <u>The servant was following the Lord</u> and the Lord directed his steps. <u>Psalms 37:23, Proverbs 3:6.</u> The Lord leads us along the path a step at a time, but before He can lead us along the path we must be on the path. When a Christian is doing the will of God, as best he/she knows it and is willing to do His further will even before he knows it, then he will know His will as soon as he needs to. <u>John 7:17.</u>

Verse 27

If our lives are surrendered to Him, He will always lead us. The world can say what they will but we know that God is working all things after the counsel of His will. To be in God's will and know it is to experience <u>joy.</u>

Verse 28

Rebekah had to run and ask her father Bethuel and her brother Laban whether it would all right for them to spend the night. Rebekah first went to her mother, to whom she probably felt closer to.

Verse 29-31

The world welcome's the Christian when it sees gold. Laban worshiped idols. <u>31:30.</u> Don't be deceived by the world and their praise. They are in the flesh and cannot please God. <u>Romans 8:7-8.</u> It takes gold to please Laban. It takes a surrendered heart to please God.

Verse 31-33

To have everyone taken care of the camels, the men it was a blessing to get washed up and sit in a home and eat a good meal was of great encouragement to Abraham's servant.

Verse 33

But the business of our Lord takes priority; everything else must take second place. More urgent than food is the work of God. When work is to be done for the Lord, He sustains us, <u>Isaiah 40:31.</u> Sometimes He makes us lie down in green pastures and lead's us beside waters, at other times the King's business takes away appetite. <u>John 4:32-34.</u>

It was customary to leave business until after the meal. Rebekah and her family were equally anxious to know what he had come for, and so when Abraham's servant said, in verse 33, "I will not eat until I have told mine errand." They told him, by all means, go ahead.

Verse 34-36

Here we have the servant's testimony concerning Abraham and Isaac. Though this is much repetition for us, it was thrilling to hear for Rebekah who was hearing these same great things for the first time.

Since this was a marriage proposal it was proper to give a statement of his master's financial status. He gave God all the credit. It was all because of God's Grace.

The servant noted that Isaac was the sole heir. Abraham turned over his fortune to Isaac in fulfillment of the promises and plan of God. Again Abraham typified God the Father and Isaac the Son of God. We know that Abraham did not love his Isaac as much as God loved His Son. Colossians 1:13, 15-19. All who reject Jesus Christ, rejects God. John 5:23. May we honor God in Christ.

Verse 37-49

Abraham's servant recounts the whole story of his mission, and gives all the details of how God led him to Rebekah, and Rebekah to him.

Abraham's Lord is still our Lord, and He does still lead His people in the right way.

Verse 50-52

After this testimony there could be no doubt that God had led the servant to select Rebekah as Isaac's bride. Both her father and her brother, Bethuel and Laban immediately acknowledged that regardless of their personal feelings in the matter. No doubt they were not completely happy to have Rebekah go so far from home. The father's permission had to be sought, as well as the brothers in this case. When the consent was given as Abraham would have done had he been present, the servant prostrated himself to the ground and worshiped the Lord.

When the Lord sets out to perform a work, it will be accomplished, and even the unregenerate admit that His hand was in it. You know we have opportunity to produce that effect. Matthew 5:16.

Abraham's servant had let his light shine so clearly that Laban and his family had to admit that the matter came from the Lord. How wonderful it is when we know we are in the will of God! We can step out into the dark if we know He is leading.

Verse 53

There are gifts for the bride even before she has seen the bridegroom. We have the Holy Spirit, the Word of God. We have the gifts of pardon, peace, purity power, hope and most of all, we have Him. Romans 8:32.

"…he gave also to her brother and to her mother precious things." The people of the world are blessed even if they do not receive the Lord Jesus personally. Matthew 5:45. God is so good! Amen. He is good to all. Acts 27:22, Romans 2:4. Lord thank you for the patience of Thy love.

Verse 54-55

The servant surprised everyone by requesting

an <u>immediate departure.</u> Rebekah's mother and brother were naturally upset by this request. They had willingly given their consent for Rebekah to go, <u>but so soon!</u> The servant had good reason for his request. The Lord had clearly indicated His leading there should be no delay in following His will. <u>Delay</u> would give the flesh <u>the opportunity to find reasons for rethinking the decision, and possibly changing it.</u> We are pilgrims and God will never allow us to forget it. Here we have no continuing city. <u>Procrastination</u> is a thief of time and rewards.

Verse 56-58

<u>"...Hinder me not..."</u> We are not to hinder the precious Holy Spirit. We are to obey His leading <u>now.</u>

Rebekah was ready to go immediately. Her decision was right. We are not to get ahead of the Lord, <u>but</u> we are not to lag behind. Delay can only be dangerous, <u>II Corinthians 6:2,</u> for Salvation, and for the Christian concerning the will of God. "Lord may we love Thee as Thou hast loved us."

Verse 59-61

One can only imagine what was going on in Rebekah's mind as she makes the long hard trip back.

She <u>"followed the man,"</u> the servant kept an eye upon Rebekah making sure she was all right. He may have told her about Isaac. The Holy Spirit whispers to us of Christ. The Holy Spirit is the comforter (called along side of). He accompanies the church through the world's wilderness teaching and showing us the things of Christ.

Verse 62-69

It is good to meditate, pray, to be alone. What a must it is to be alone with God.

Verse 65

"...she took a vail and covered herself..." A token of humility, modesty and subjection.

Verse 66-67

He brought her to his mother's tent, and was married. It had been three years since his mother died. How fulfilling marriage is when in the will of God, both physically and spiritually. A man who truly loves and honors his father and mother will when the time comes for marriage, likewise love and honor his wife.

What a meeting this was for Isaac and Rebekah. What a meeting it will be for us who love the Lord. I Thessalonians 4:16-17.

Chapter 25

Verse 1-4

We do not know much on <u>Keturah</u>, the scripture is silent. She is referred to in

<u>I Chronicles 1:32.</u> This seems to be a fleshy mistake of Abraham. Of the six sons' of Keturah and Abraham, <u>Midian</u> and his descendants are mentioned often in the Old Testament as a <u>thorn to Israel</u>. The Midianites at times, seem to have been allied with the <u>Ishmaelites.</u> <u>Genesis37:25-28, 36,</u> the Moabites, <u>Numbers 25:1, 6-15</u> and the Amalekites, <u>Judges 6:3.</u>

Keturah must have understood when she married Abraham that Isaac would have the inheritance, although her children would be provided for. <u>Abraham lived 35 years after Isaac's marriage.</u>

Verse 5-6

All these descendants of Abraham from his <u>concubines</u>, gradually merged and become the modern day Arabic people. Before Abraham died he bestowed gifts upon his descendants; <u>but the bulk of it all went to Isaac.</u>

Verse 7-10

Here we have recorded the end of a remarkable life. <u>Abraham was 175 yeas old.</u> He was buried where Sarah was buried. <u>Psalms 91:15-16.</u> Abraham was satisfied with his days; <u>his life had been fulfilled with God.</u>

So far as we know this is the last act that these half-brothers performed together. Until this day the Arab's fight Jews.

Verse 11

<u>Isaac was now the only surviving link in the Messianic line.</u> <u>Isaac is a double portrait of sonship.</u> Not only does he portray the Son of the Father, but he also represents our own sonship with the Father. Just as Abraham gave all that he had to Isaac, so God appointed Christ heir of all things, <u>Hebrews 1:2.</u> We are the children of Abraham by faith, and are thus <u>the children of God.</u> <u>Romans 8:17.</u> God is willing to bless us even as He blessed Isaac. All the wealth of the Father and of the Son becomes ours <u>through our sonship.</u> <u>Romans 8:32.</u>

"...and Isaac dwelt by the well Lahai-roi." Abraham was a man <u>of alters</u>, Jacob a <u>man of tents,</u> but Isaac was a <u>man of wells.</u> Abraham lived in Ur and Egypt, Jacob dwelt in Egypt, but Isaac never left the land of blessing. On seven occasions Isaac is mentioned in connection with wells. The well is the symbol of the water of life. Happy is the believer who learns to dwell there.

Verse 12-18

God took the trouble to record the names of

the twelve sons' of Ishmael because they were the grandson's of Abraham. They were to be blessed because God had promised. <u>Genesis 17:20.</u> Ishmael was 137 years old.

Verse 19-23

Isaac was 40 years old when he married Rebekah, and it would be another 20 years before they would have any children. <u>Genesis 25:20, 26.</u> Like Abraham and Sarah they had to wait many years and to make it a matter of special prayer, before God sent them a son. Isaac well knew God's promises concerning the seed that would come through him, but perhaps he took them too much for granted. Twenty years of bareness, <u>drove him to prayer</u> that he and Rebekah might have a child. <u>God desires for us to pray for the supply of our needs, and His blessings</u>, even though He has already promised to send them. <u>Matthew 6:11, 7:11, Philippians 4:19.</u>

Verse 23

<u>A problem soon developed within the womb, there began to be a conflict between the two boys.</u> Rebekah began to realize that something was going on, and so she went before the Lord with her problem. And the Lord gave her an answer. <u>The twins had problems in the womb, and the two nations that they became had problems. God is sovereign. The elder son would serve the younger.</u> The children not

yet born, not having done good or evil, shows that God is sovereign and that the purpose of God is not in works, but all of God.

It was in days of old that the eldest son received the greater honor and inheritance, but God does not necessarily work that way. <u>Seth, Isaac, Jacob, Judah, and David, none of them were first born sons.</u> One of the two sons in Rebekah's womb would carry on the Messianic line, and God said it would be the younger. Neither Isaac nor Jacob were the first born. <u>God is sovereign and is not to be questioned as to His choices. Daniel 4:35.</u>

Verse 24-26

When the twins were born, the first one to emerge from the womb was red and hairy, the second, light and smooth. Apparently they were still struggling even as they were born, because the second was hanging on with his hand to the heel of the first, as though trying to pull him back. <u>Hosea 12:3. This baby became Israel – prince with God.</u> Although God had to discipline Jacob for his folly in his schemes, he was greatly blessed of God.

At first he grasped in the flesh, but eventually he grasped the things which the Lord had for him.

Verse 27-34

<u>Esau,</u> he was intent only on present gratification, and set no value on the divine gifts. He preferred

playing out in the field, to working for his family and serving the Lord. Hebrews 12:16.

Notice Hebrews 11:9. He did this because he was a man of faith, to whom God's plans and promises meant far more than physical pleasure. Everybody in the family, that is Jacob and Rebekah could see that it would have been tragic for Esau to get the blessing, as he was neither interested in God's promise nor qualified to transfer them to his own children.

The eldest son customarily received a double portion of the inheritance. Deuteronomy 21:17. This was the custom at the time, but was not yet a Biblical Law. The father had the privilege of transferring it from the eldest son to another.

I Chronicles 5:1-2.

Jacob thought, would Esau sell his birthright for some chili? Jacob should have been willing to let God work out the problem. Jacob's sin was lack of faith, and he estranged himself from his family, instead of winning them. Wait on God and let Him work it out. He wanted spiritual blessing, even though he went the wrong way to obtain them.

CHAPTER 26

Verse 1

A famine. Isaac had never experienced such a thing, and it was beginning to be disastrous for his flocks and herds.

A test. Always a test, feast or famine, evil or good. Just as every coin shows head and tail, so every test of life reveals the possibility of spiritual growth or spiritual decline.

When prosperity comes do we become selfish, or do we joyfully praise God? In time of famine do we despair, or do we draw closer to the Lord? Romans 8:35.

"...Isaac went unto Abimelech..." Isaac was going ahead of God instead of resting in faith. To walk by sight always leads to further trials and falls.

This chapter is exclusively devoted to Isaac, and there are many things to learn from this chapter. Romans 15:4. Isaac was the ordinary son of a famous father, and the ordinary father of a famous son. We will find in this chapter Isaac having the covenant confirmed to him. We will notice how the sins of the father repeat themselves in the children. Isaac went down; he walked by sight rather than by faith. We also find again Isaac and wells.

Verse 2

This is the first time God appeared to Isaac since he was on Mt. Moriah with his father Abraham. He was planning to go down further to Egypt when the Lord stopped him. <u>Oh how faithful God is to us.</u> What Grace, that God should appear when we are out of His will, and keep us from going further down. God said <u>"...Go not down..."</u> Like so many of us, Isaac looked down, not up. Not Egypt, <u>Egypt glitters, but God is not there</u>. Let us pray, "Lord, lead us to Thy dwelling."

Verse 3-4

<u>The Lord had not forgotten His covenant concerning Isaac.</u> He at this time repeated it to Isaac. God says don't leave this land. <u>"Sojourn in this land, and I will be with thee..."</u> This 26th chapter is the only chapter that tells much of Isaac. Was there any cause in Isaac for God to bless him? <u>None!</u>

Isaac lived longer than his father and his son, and much less is told of him. "The ordinary life is the ordered life, but the fact that the Lord dwelt with him made it extraordinary."

<u>"...unto thee, and unto thy seed..."</u> Isaac was ordinary but in view of God's plan we see his vital importance. <u>Galatians 3:16.</u> Isaac is great because the seed in his loins will bring forth the Messiah.

All the land was Isaac's through God's covenant

to Abraham. Just think all the promises made to the believers of all ages are the same promises given to you and me. <u>Amen!</u>

Verse 5

After Abraham was justified, he sought to walk in God's ways. God was pleased with Abraham and used his life to rebuke Isaac.

<u>Notice the word "My" used five times.</u> "...my voice..." His voice is to be heard and believed, "faith cometh by hearing, and hearing by the Word of God. "<u>...my charge...</u>" His charge is to be kept, and observed. "<u>...my commandments...</u>" His commandments are to be obeyed. "<u>...my statutes...</u>" His statutes are to be acknowledged. "<u>...my laws...</u>" His laws are to be followed. He cannot but bless those who give heed to all that He is. <u>"What Abraham heard from God, he obeyed."</u>

Verse 6

Gerar was a part of Canaan but was controlled by a colony of Philistines. <u>The Kings</u>, or Abimelech, of this colony was not the same one that Abraham knew, but no doubt he had heard of Abraham.

Verse 7

Isaac knew of his father's sin, but no doubt the memory grew dim, and he found himself repeating the same lie Abraham used. <u>Genesis 12:13, 20:12.</u>

Oh what danger Isaac placed Rebekah in. <u>Thank God for His Grace.</u> God had chosen, Sarah and Rebekah to be mothers in the line of the Messiah.

Verse 8

Abimelech looked out at a window. Very little is hidden from the world. When a Christian disobeys God, a worldling is watching from some window. <u>Matthew 5:16.</u> How unfortunate when the world can use our actions to blaspheme the name of God. <u>Romans 2:23-24, I Timothy 6:1, Titus 2:5.</u>

Verse 9

When Abimelech confronted Isaac, Isaac had to admit what he had done and why he had done it. <u>The only thing a believer can do is to acknowledge sin and repent.</u> Is there anything sadder in this world than that a child of God should be rebuked by a man of the world. <u>We should have a healthy fear of sin.</u>

Verse 10

<u>All sin affects those around us.</u> Although Isaac's deception was not intended to hurt Abimelech, it was a great sin against him. <u>It made Adultery possible</u>. Let's pray, <u>"Lord make us aware of the danger of sin."</u> Again, God kept the men away from Rebekah.

Verse 11

Abimelech, instead of taking vengeance on Isaac for his deception, pronounced a penalty for any of his people who harmed either Isaac or Rebekah. <u>We see the providence of God</u>, who promised to bless those who blessed Abraham and his seed, and to curse those who cursed them. Now Abraham's son got into trouble of his own making. <u>God intervened</u> and caused a pagan king to issue a ruling to protect Isaac and Rebekah. Abimelech protected the very people who would destroy the Philistines one day. <u>Proverbs 21:1.</u>

Verse 12

Here is the <u>first mention of seed sowing in the Bible.</u> The Lord blessed it a hundred fold. Seed sowing in the New Testament is symbolic of witnessing.

In the parable of the sower we see the good seed, brought forth a hundred fold. <u>Matthew 13:23.</u>

God blessed Isaac. <u>Thank God for this truth in Psalms 130:3.</u> The wonderful fact is that God always deals with His people <u>in Grace.</u> Amen!

Verse 13

The blessing of the Lord brought a beautiful harvest for Isaac. The Lord does not always give material prosperity as the mark of His Grace. Some of His most blessed people are troubled. <u>God works with Job as well as with Isaac.</u> <u>Philippians 4:12, Hebrews 11:32-40.</u>

Verse 14

Isaac prospered so much that the Philistines envied him. Envy is everywhere but lets notice what God says in I Timothy 6:6, Lord give us godliness with contentment. Amen.

Verse 15-16

An adequate supply of water was needed for Isaac's prosperity to continue. He had water because of the wells his father dug. The Philistines decided to plug up these wells and to force Isaac out of their country.

In scripture wells symbolize the Word of God, from which our blessings come. The devil will seek to stop the wells of those who have been saved. Many things can choke our wells. D.L. Moody had in the front of his Bible, "This Book will keep you from sin, and sin will keep you from this Book." Pray, Lord, let Thy Word flow powerfully.

Verse 17

Isaac could have resisted the demand in verse 16. Earlier Abimelech had given Abraham the right to dwell anywhere he wanted. Genesis 20:15. The wells belonged to Abraham by right of construction Isaac moved from the capital city, going east in the valley of Gerar.

Verse 18

Isaac began a well reopening campaign. Isaac instead of going back to the land God had given to his father, he remains in Gerar. It appears that Isaac is not walking close with God. Because he remains in the land we see trouble for him, Jeremiah 6:16.

Verse 19

Isaac's servants dig another well and find an artesian well.

Verse 20

The Philistine herdsman claimed the water. Isaac instead of fighting went on. He called the well, "Esek" – The Quarrel well.

Verse 21

We have more conflict. Sitnah – "The hatred Well" – opposition.

Isaac had to have water, and God gave it to him, but Isaac was not where God wanted him to be, God gave him strife with it. Both water and the contention were from the Lord. Whenever blessing is mixed with contention, perhaps we are not completely in the will of God. To those who are in the center of His will there is no sorrow. Proverbs 10:22.

Verse 22

Rehoboth – "The well of Ample Room." Actually, Isaac was cramped by being out of the will of

God. How many Christians live on the border of spiritually, thinking they have arrived? Pray, "Lord give us discernment."

Verse 23

Year's before Abraham made a covenant with the Philistines at Beersheba, <u>Genesis 21:32-34.</u> Isaac had lived there after the sacrifice on Mt. Moriah, <u>Genesis 22:19.</u> And so home at last.

Verse 24

God graciously met him the very first night he was back in Beersheba. The ways of God are wonderful. Here we see the forgiving father waiting at the gate looking down the road watching for the prodigal son who has been in the far country.

God is a faithful, covenant keeping God. He blesses us, not because we deserve it, but simply because He has set His love upon us. <u>II Timothy 2:13.</u> God was with Isaac and would keep His promises, for Abraham's sake, God assures Isaac of His presence. Oh how wonderful He is!

Verse 25

This appears to be the only Alter Isaac builds himself. Isaac calls upon the name of the Lord. Prayer follows his return. Sacrifice and prayer. And he dug another well. And the waters of blessing gush forth. "Lord may we abide and dig."

Verse 26

The King himself comes to Isaac with a delegation. They know Jehovah was blessing Isaac, and that he was growing stronger all the time. They decided it was wise to stay on good terms with Isaac.

When the Christian is in the will of God and blessing is flowing from him, those round about will soon perceive his friendship and prevailing power with God. John 7:38.

Isaac was back in the land with an alter and a well, Abimelech came to him. You cannot win your unsaved friends and relatives by living like them, but you can win them by being like Christ.

Verse 27

We notice that Isaac was bold as he spoke with the Philistines, as he was fortified with God's promise. When you are in the will of God, and filled with His Holy Spirit, you will have Holy Spirit Boldness to do right, to speak for Christ.

Verse 28

Again even the heathen, "saw certainly that the LORD was with thee..." They knew the advantage of doing business with one who was blessed by God.

Verse 29

They reminded him that they had not harmed

him or Rebekah, and that they had prospered greatly in their land. So they proposed a <u>nonaggressive</u>
<u>treaty.</u>

Verse 30-31

Isaac was agreeable to this and <u>hosted a feast.</u>
In that culture, to eat with others is to make strong
friendships. <u>Genesis 21:25-31.</u>

Verse 32-33

Isaac's servants came to him with this happy
news, that the well they were digging had struck a
good supply of water - Beersheba – <u>"The well of the</u>
<u>oath."</u>

This is a missionary story. Israel should be a missionary people, for the <u>promise </u>was that <u>all families</u>
and <u>all nations</u> would be blessed in them.

God never meant for them to clutch the blessing to themselves. And so here at Beersheba we remember our obligation to the whole world. <u>We are</u>
<u>debtors.</u> <u>Romans 1:14-15.</u>

Verse 34-35

Isaac was at <u>peace with his neighbors</u> but he had
<u>war at home.</u> His worldly son <u>Esau</u> had married two
heathen wives who caused grief to Isaac and Rebekah. Later, just to provoke his parents, he married
a third heathen wife. <u>Genesis 28:8-9.</u>

There are few grief's greater then to see loved

ones unequally yoked with unbelievers. A mixed marriage can never be true, but <u>will always draw the believer away from fellowship with the Lord.</u>

<u>Nothing is more conducive to spiritual decline then the unequal yoke.</u>

<u>II Corinthians 6:14-18.</u>

Chapter 27

Here we have a family that fell apart. Isaac did not end right. "A good beginning doesn't guarantee a good ending." This is taught in Scripture, through the lives of Lot, Samson, King Saul, King Solomon, Demus and Isaac.

If ever a man was blessed with a great beginning, it was Isaac. Yet he ended his life under a cloud.

Verse 1-4

He put himself ahead of the Lord. Isaac thought he was going to die soon, and yet his greatest desire was to enjoy a good meal at the hand of his favorite son, and cook, Esau. Genesis 25:28

When Abraham prepared for death, his concern was to get a bride for his son. When King David came to the end of his life, he made arrangements for the building of the temple, Paul's burden before his martyrdom was that Timothy be faithful to preach the Word.

Isaac instead of working to bring his family closer together wanted only one thing, a savory meal of venison. There was favoritism in the family. He disobeyed God's command. Before the boy's were born, God had told Isaac and Rebekah that Jacob, the younger son, was to receive the covenant blessing. Genesis 25:19-23. Yet Isaac planned to give the blessing to Esau. Isaac knew that Esau had despised his birthright and sold it to Jacob, and that <u>Esau had disqualified himself by marrying a heathen woman.</u>

Isaac lived by his feelings. Isaac was blind and apparently bedfast, a condition you would think would make him <u>trust God and seek His help.</u> Instead, Isaac rejected the way of faith and depended on his own senses, <u>Taste, verse 4, 9, & 25. Touch, verse 21, Hearing verse 22</u> and <u>Smell, verse 27.</u> He did not take the way of faith. <u>Proverbs 19:21.</u> Most people today would endorse the idea of making their decisions on the basis of how they feel and not what God says in His Word. <u>"If it feels good, it is good." They say!</u>

Isaac was a declining believer, living by the natural instead of the supernatural, and trusting his own senses instead of believing and obeying the Word of God.

When we think of all that resulted from Isaac's fleshly hunger, Esau went hunting, Rebekah had Jacob deceive his father, Esau's hatred was aroused and Jacob was forced to flee. <u>We can see how important it is to be careful, and suppress fleshly desires. Philippians 3:18-19.</u> There are many who profess Christ, but are enemies to Christ's cross. <u>Their walk is a surer evidence of what they are, than their profession. Matthew 7:20-21.</u> They mind nothing but their sensual appetites, and lived to fulfill them.

How dishonoring to Christ for a Christian to live this way. It is a sad thing when the body is allowed to dominate the soul. I Corinthians 9:27. May we pray, "Lord put a guard on all our appetites."

Verse 5-17

Sir Walter Scott – "O what a tangled web we weave, when first we practice to deceive."

Faith is living without scheming, faith means obeying God no matter how we feel, what we think or what might happen. The obedience of faith was the secret of Abraham's life. Hebrews 11:8. The absence of obedient faith brought trouble to the home of Isaac and Rebekah.

Verse 5

Rebekah was a deceitful, proud, selfish woman who wanted her way and not the Lord's. Her eavesdropping was for her advantage. She showed lack of faith in the Lord's promise, if she had been willing to wait, He would have given the birthright blessing in His own time and way. Never does the end justify the means. Rebekah and Jacob had no right to do evil that good might come. It is tragic when husband and wife no longer discuss God's Word or pray together.

Scheming. Knowing that Jacob was chosen to receive the covenant blessing, Rebekah took matters into her own hands to make sure her favorite son got what the Lord had promised him. <u>Lack of faith is not good.</u> Isaac was depending on his own physical senses, and Rebekah was depending on the wisdom of the world. <u>James 3:13-18.</u>

Verse 11

Jacob's concern wasn't, "<u>Is it right?</u>" But "<u>Is it safe?</u>" He was worried about the 11th commandment, "<u>Thou shalt not get caught.</u>" Little did she know that when Jacob left for Haran, she would never see her favorite son again.

<u>Isaac</u>, "if it feels good, it is good."

<u>Rebekah</u>, "the end justifies the means."
Rebekah couldn't trust God to fulfill His plan; she had to help God out because it was for a good cause. But there is no place for deception in the life of the believer, for Satan is the deceiver, <u>II Corinthians 11:3,</u> Jesus Christ is truth, <u>John 14:6, Psalms 32:2.</u>

Verse 18-29

Jacob was weaving a tangled web; he just kept on with deceit, and more deceit. One lie led to another.

Verse 18-19

<u>He lied about his name.</u> We see that Isaac was becoming suspicious, he did not expect Esau to return so quickly from the hunt and the voice he heard didn't sound like the voice of Esau. That is when Jacob told his first lie, he claimed to be Esau.

Verse 19-20

<u>He lied about the food and the Lord.</u> He claimed to have obeyed his father's wishes (lie #2); he called the goat's meat "my game" (lie #3). He gave credit to the Lord for helping him find it so quickly (lie #4), he not only lied about himself, but he also lied about the Lord. To use the Lord to cover up sin is <u>blasphemy.</u> Few stop at one lie, and how terrible to add blasphemy to lying.

Verse 21-27

<u>He lied again about his identity and about his love.</u>

Isaac felt Jacob's hand and mistook goat skin for human hair and Jacob assured him again that he indeed was Esau (lie #5).

After Isaac had eaten the meal, he asked Jacob to kiss him, and that kiss was the (lie #6), for it was hypocritical. <u>Luke 22:48.</u>

Since the smell of the garments finally convinced Isaac that Esau was there, everything was set for the giving of the blessing. Isaac blessed Jacob with natural and material wealth.

Verse 28-29

He quoted the Lord's original promise to Abraham, 12:3, it was done. Isaac could not revoke the blessing. Three things Jacob is blessed with, 1. Plenty, 2. Power, 3. Prevalence with God. <u>"... cursed *be* every</u>

one that curseth thee, and blessed *be* he that blesseth thee."

Verse 30-33

Why was Isaac so moved? Because he knew that the Lord had over ruled his selfish plan so that his favorite son did not get the blessing. Isaac had lied to Abimelech in chapter 26, and he had tried to lie to God by disobeying the Word, but now his own lies had caught up with him.

Verse 34-40

The man who despised his birthright and married two pagan women now weeps and cries out for his father to bless him.

Hebrews 12:16-17. Esau tried to repent, his heart was hard; and he couldn't change what was done. Esau's tears were not tears of repentance for being an ungodly man; they were tears of regret because he had lost the covenant blessing. "Esau wanted the covenant blessing but he didn't want to be the kind of man whom God could bless."

Verse 39-40

Isaac reaffirmed the word God gave about the boys.

If God were able to make a saint out of such material as this He also can take our poor lives with the sin and failure and make something of it for His glory.

Verse 41

"Don't get mad, get even." Esau carried both; he carried a hateful grudge against his brother and planned to kill him. The man who was to live by the sword started at home. This is a picture of the world hating the true church. John 15:19. Such hatred manifested by Esau is rebellion against God. Is God not sovereign? Can He not do as He pleases? We recognize the right of a general to send one man into battle to death or glory, and another to unload freight. Why should we not acknowledge the sovereignty of God?

Esau wanted to kill Jacob. Why does one man desire to murder another? It is a mad cry from his rebellious heart. God He can't do that to me. You should be running things to suit me. The taking of life is the prerogative of God. The Bible tells us that thoughts of hatred come from a murderous heart. I John 3:15.

Esau supposed his father was near death, but he lived another 40 years after.

Verse 42

Rebekah had heard of Esau's plans to kill Jacob, perhaps Esau uttered his plans in the hearing of some servants. Proverbs 29:11.

Verse 43

Rebekah again takes matters into her own hands,

and quickly makes her plans, <u>she assumed</u> that she could just send Jacob away for a few days and then everything would be all right. <u>This is a picture of sowing in the flesh.</u> <u>Galatians 6:7- 8.</u>

There was more than one reason for sending Jacob to his relatives which we will see in a moment.

Verse 44

<u>"...a few days..."</u> turned out to be <u>20 years.</u> Rebekah never saw her favorite son again. Her scheming cost her a great price. Sometimes we buy things at a bargain and it ends up costing much more. <u>"This is always true of sin,"</u> <u>sin in the home always brings heartache.</u> Had Isaac and Rebekah not taken sides with their boys, had they continued to pray about matters as in their early married life, had they allowed God to have His way, then affairs would have been different. <u>Instead, all of them suffered because of unbelief and disobedience.</u>

Verse 45

Poor Rebekah, Jacob fled and Esau departed. She feared that Esau would murder Jacob and in turn would be killed. <u>Genesis 9:6.</u>

Verse 46

Remember Esau had married heathen women, already sorrow was in the home. How could scheming Rebekah talk Isaac into sending Jacob away?

What better way then to tell him that Jacob needs a proper wife. Again we see her almost complete <u>lack of faith</u> in the promises of God.

<u>Remember God's hand was upon Jacob. "Lord, keep us from doubting Thee."</u>

<u>Mixed marriage</u> is completely foreign to the Word of God. Marriage symbolizes the union of the believer with the Lord Jesus Christ, as the bride is joined to the bridegroom. <u>Ephesians 5:21-33.</u> The believer has <u>two natures</u>, the <u>unbeliever one. II Cor</u><u>inthians 6:14-17.</u>

Jacob supplanted (deceived), Esau twice, how? 1. He took away the <u>birthright</u>. 2. He took away the <u>blessing</u>. Remember it was God's plan for Jacob to be blessed far before the boy's were born.

<u>I Corinthians 1:26.</u> Serves as a judgment on <u>Genesis 27.</u> Here we have God's chosen family, deceiving and hurting one another, and asserting their own will in the face of His plans for them. In all the bitterness, hatred and so on which resulted in punishment, the Divine Plan was not in frustration for a moment. All four people were to blame, Isaac, Rebekah, Esau and Jacob.

CHAPTER 28

Verse 1

Isaac called Jacob, and gave him instructions not to marry a Canaanite woman, just as his father had in Genesis 24:3. Note: Matthew 18:20. Whenever two believers are joined together in marriage it is the perfect gathering of two in the name of the Lord, and He is there. This makes a true home.

Those who have the blessing must keep the charge. Deuteronomy7:1-4.

Verse 2

Jacob was to go back to his mother's family in Padanaram and there take a wife from among his own cousins, the daughters of his mother's brother. In essence Jacob must seek a wife from daughters of Shem, the line of blessing. Isaac showed some spiritual stature, it was good for Jacob to leave home to seek a wife.

Verse 3-4

Isaac repeated the blessing, as he had received it from his father. Genesis 26:3-5, Genesis 12:1-3.

"God Almighty" – Hebrew – El Shaddai, the name which God revealed to Abraham in Genesis 17:1-2. Abraham had taught its meaning to Isaac, and Isaac passed it along to Jacob. These men, Abraham, Isaac and Jacob had a great sense of the meaning of the covenant. Isaac completely in the will of the Lord gave his son the blessing of the covenant.

All the principals of divine blessing were tied up in the Abrahamic Covenant. Every born again believer of any generation has been blessed by this covenant. Galatians 3:14.

Verse 5

This separation was to be for a short while, but instead lasted for 20 years. Our future is safe in the Hands of God. God has hidden from us the immediate future and has revealed to us the glorious eternal future, God is so merciful.

Isaac and Rebekah believed that Jacob could find a wife that believed in Jehovah among their own kin.

Verse 6-9

Esau knew now that Jacob indeed had the blessing and that Isaac and Rebakah were behind Jacob. Esau in an attempt to partially correct the situation (to late) went to his uncle Ishmael's family and got one of his daughters to marry. But, Ishmael's line was the wrong line. Esau had been spiritually blind and stubborn about this all important issue of the right wife, but now that it was too late, he made a last desperate attempt to regain the favor of his parents.

The devil is an imitator. The blessing of God on a believer sometimes brings imitation of the unbeliever. Many unsaved people imitate believers. Griffith Thomas, "He will not do precisely what God requires, but something like it. He will not entirely give up the world and put God first in his life, but he will try to meet some of God's wishes by a little alteration in his conduct. Instead of renouncing sin he will cover it with the glory of small virtues; but it is one thing to conform to the outward practices of God's people, it is quite another to be thoroughly and truly godly at heart."

So Esau goes out and marries the daughter of Ishmael. He thinks it will please his father. You see what a lack of spiritual perception he has. The Ishmaelites were as much rejected as the Canaanites or the Philistines. It was the Ishmaelites who bought Joseph and sold him to Potiphar. Genesis 37:28.

Verse 7

Although we have seen the disobedience of this family, the deceit, and weakness, we also see the Hand of God. We see a display of God's Grace and Power on our behalf. God says, "Be still, and know that I *am* God ..." Philippians 4:5-7. God graciously overrules our folly and weakness, and while we are called upon to reap the fruits of our unbelieving and impatient ways, He takes this and teaches us lessons of His grace and wisdom.

God is above all, and can bring good out of evil. Jacob left home with his father's blessing, but had a lot to learn about God, for himself. <u>In Jacob's dark hour, he finds God.</u> Sometimes God has to bring us to the end of ourselves before He can reach into our hearts and do great things, as with Jacob having to leave home. <u>F.B. Meyer said;</u> "Often our nest is broken up that we may learn to fly."

Verse 10

Jacob was a home boy; he had spent most of his life at Beersheba. <u>Genesis 22:19, 26:33, 28:10.</u> It was 500 miles to Haran. He was fleeing from an <u>angry brother</u>, and facing an <u>unknown future</u>, but he had his father's blessing. From now on the homeboy would have to become <u>a pilgrim</u> and <u>walk by faith</u> when he decided to spend the night at Bethel, he had no idea that God would meet him there, and from that night at <u>Bethel was a very special place to Jacob.</u> God has plans and purposes for His children. <u>One of the most important truths for every Christian to learn is that God has a plan for his/her life.</u> May we then pray, "Lord, help me to face the unknown with trust."

Verse 11

Jacob slept on the earth with a stone for his pillow. This verse says, "And he lighted upon a certain place..." It was a very special place, <u>Bethel.</u> It was here that Abraham built an altar. <u>Genesis 12:8, 13:3-4.</u> This place was a special place to the Patriarch fathers. It was at this place that God chose to make Himself personally known to Jacob, as He had been known to Abraham, and to Isaac. May we pray, "Lord, daily reveal Thyself to us." <u>Stone pillow,</u> remember that Jacob was on the run, and although God's plan was not stopped by Jacob and his families' disobedience, Jacob was like what we read in <u>Proverbs 13:15.</u>

Verse 12

Jacob had known and believed God's promises, and no doubt worshiped the Lord and prayed to Him. But never before had God actually appeared and spoken to him. What we have here is a <u>theophany</u> – a pre-Bethlehem appearance of Jesus Christ.

In this dream it shows there is an intense interest in heaven concerning what takes place on earth. <u>About angels,</u> <u>Hebrews 1:14, Hebrews 12:22, Psalms 103:20, Psalms 91:11, Psalms 34:7, I Peter1:12, I Corinthians 4:9, Luke 15:10.</u>

<u>This ladder</u> also showed Jacob that there is a way from earth to heaven and that is through <u>the Lord Jesus Christ.</u> God reveals Himself to sinners. Thank and Praise His name!

The Lord Jesus Christ glorified the Father on

earth. John 17:4. Jesus delivered us from bondage. Amen! Romans 8:21, Habakkuk 2:14. Only God's ladder can reach to heaven. This was a dream that Jacob had, but it was a dream symbolizing a marvelous reality. Remember dreams as well as visions was just two of the ways that God revealed Himself to man. Hebrews 1:1. How does God reveal Himself to man in the New Testament, or the Church Age? Bible, who is the ladder? Jesus. John 1:51, 3:13.

Verse 13

When Jacob saw the Lord, and heard Him, notice he did not rebuke Jacob, but blessed him and gave the promise again. Oh what assurance. There is no loneliness that the Lord cannot take care of, no need that He cannot meet. If the believer but realizes that the Lord wants to be all things to him, and do all things for him, his life will become what the Lord wishes it to be. Our Lord is far more eager to bless than we are to be blessed. Life is the process of growing up and learning, often the hard way, that our own choices are not best. When we see the Lord, He becomes all.

Verse 14

"And thy seed shall be as the dust of the earth, and thou shalt spread abroad..." Here is the true reason for anti-Semitism. All the forces of Satan are set against the plan of God. The Lord Jesus told believers that if they were of the world, the world would love them, but because they are not the world would hate them, John 15:19. The same is true of Israel, the chosen people.

"...in thy seed shall all the families of the earth be blessed." This is why the Lord chose Israel. Deuteronomy7:6-8. The reason was that from this people would come the line of Jesus Christ.

Verse 15

This passage should convince us that the Lord blesses us not because of anything in ourselves, but because He has been pleased to set His love upon us. See Jacob fleeing the consequences of his trickery. The Lord does not give us what we deserve. At Calvary the Father put upon Jesus all that we deserve so that He might put on us all that Christ deserves.

"And will keep thee in all places..." The Lord promised to keep Jacob wherever he went. Oh what abundant Grace!

"I will not leave thee..." Most precious of all promises is that of the presence of the Lord. It was made to Jacob in pure grace. To Moses in Deuteronomy 31:6, to Joshua in Joshua 1:5, 8, to Solomon in I Chronicles 28:20, to the disciples in Matthew 28:20, and confirmed today in Hebrews 13:5. The guiding and abiding presence of the Lord enables us to claim, Hebrews 13:6.

Verse 16

After God had finished speaking, Jacob awoke in awe. He had <u>actually met God</u> in this place. He awoke and his first response was surprise. Are you aware that God is actually with you at this moment? The Lord has put you where you are, in order to be gracious to you.

Verse 17

When he awoke not only was he surprised, but he was afraid. <u>Proverbs 1:7.</u> This is good; when the soul comes into contact with God the result is awe, reverence and fear.

"...How dreadful *is* this place!..." This word dreadful means reverence or awe. <u>Lord</u>, <u>give us holy</u> <u>reverential awe of Thee!</u>

"...<u>the house of God...</u> There was no building. In our day because the Holy Spirit dwells in believers, wherever we are is the house of God or The Temple. <u>John 14:17.</u> Jacob would be away from his father's house for 20 years, <u>but</u> the Lord would be his dwelling place. <u>Psalms 90:1.</u>

Verse 18

Jacob got up early, <u>he had something to do.</u> He took care to preserve the memorial of it. He set up a stone for a pillar and poured oil upon it. This anointing of objects was for to set apart for sacred uses. Jacob did this in <u>gratitude</u> to God for this vision.

The pouring out of liquid (oil) was symbolic of pouring ones life out in devotion to the Lord. <u>Exodus 29:38 - 41, Philippians 2:17, II Corinthians 12:15.</u>

Verse 19

"<u>Beth</u>" – House, "<u>El</u>" – <u>God</u>. Bethel, House of God. Jacob recognized that the Lord had met with him. Jacob later changed the name to El-Bethel, <u>God of the House of God.</u>

All the sacredness that Jacob put on that place, we today must put to our bodies. <u>I Corinthians 6:19.</u> This is why we have <u>Romans 12:1.</u>

Verse 20

This is the <u>first vow recorded in the Bible.</u> There was nothing spiritual about it. "A vow," was promises to perform certain things for, or bring certain offerings to God, in return for certain benefits which were hoped for at His hand. Nowhere in the Old Testament do we find the making of vows regarded as a religious duty. <u>Deuteronomy 23:22.</u> A vow was as binding as an oath, and was not to be taken lightly.

Making vows to God does not make one spiritual. Vows are a result of being spiritual.

"<u>…If God be with me…</u>" All the benefits Jacob sought for had already been provided for, <u>all ready promised.</u> We should not say, "<u>God if,</u>" but rather,

"Because you have been so good, I will be wholly yours."

Verse 21

We are not to bargain with God, we must yield fully to Him. Isaiah26:13. We must acknowledge Him as our only Sovereign, whom we are to love and serve with all our heart, mind soul and strength.

Verse 22

Although the law of the tithe had not yet been established Jacob understood the principal. This as well as other divine principals were revealed to God's people long before they became legal obligations. "A tenth," under grace everything belongs to the Lord. The truly yielded soul would not be content with just 10 percent.

CHAPTER 29

Verse 1

Life isn't easy, and what life does to us depends a great deal on what life finds in us. During the next 20 years, Jacob would experience many painful trials in Laban's house hold, but he would become God's man to accomplish God's will.

This story is as up to date as this very day, for all of us are making important decisions on the road of life, decisions that determine character and destiny.

Perhaps not everybody is supposed to get married. Matthew 19:1-12, with Jacob marriage wasn't an option. The success of the covenant promises God gave to Abraham depended on Jacob's finding a wife and with her building a family that would eventually become the people of Israel, the nation that would bring the promised Redeemer.

Jacob came to Bethel with a burden; he left Bethel with the burden gone. He left in new hope and with his heart full of joy. He never forgot this night at Bethel. On his deathbed he told his sons about it. Genesis 48:3. At Bethel Jacob learned three great facts. 1. The state of his own heart. 2. His utter helplessness. 3. and the Sovereign Grace of God. Pray, "Lord, teach us to know ourselves and Thee."

We find that the Lord providentially guided Jacob to the very well where his relatives watered at.

Verse 2

Water is most important in the wilderness, lack of it means death. <u>One said,</u> "The field is the world, and the water is the Word of God." You must behold the Word of God flowing in your wilderness if you are to have <u>the freshness of the spirit.</u> Some people do not go to the Word for themselves; they build cistern's in which they store water dispensed by preacher's and teachers. This may sustain life in an anemic sort of way, but for <u>true power</u> the child of God must go beyond man to <u>behold for himself</u> the well in the field. And even then he cannot enjoy its freshness if a <u>great stone of unconfessed sin is over the well's mouth.</u>

Verse 3

Apparently the Shepherd's tending the flocks were women or young boys. The stone was too large for anyone or two of them to move. It was easier therefore to open the well once or twice a day after several would come and help each other.

Verse 4-7

Jacob suggested to them to water and to leave and feed the animals, so that he might be alone with Rachel. <u>We perhaps have love at first sight.</u> Jacob never loved any other woman; he talked about Rachel on his deathbed.

Verse 8-10

No doubt Jacob was very excited about seeing Rachel and had unusual strength and energy at this time and joy of Rachel; he single-handedly rolled away the stone. Rachel was beautiful, verse 17.

Rachel like Rebekah was willing to work and become a faithful homemaker. The flaunting, flamboyant female can never please God. I Peter 3:4.

Three times, in verse 10 mention is made of Laban, his mother's brother. Jacob not only needed a wife but a job. No doubt Jacob had heard his mother speaking fondly of her brother Laban.

Verse 11

It was the custom in this time to kiss relatives or close friends with a kiss of greeting.

Verse 12

When Jacob got a hold of himself he told Rachel who he was, he was her cousin. She now gets emotional and runs and tells her father.

Verse 13-14

When Laban heard the news he too was excited, he ran to meet him. They must have stayed up late talking. Jacob shared in the work for a month.

Verse 15

Laban offered to employ him. They were both honest and fair with each other.

Verse 16-20

Jacob did not realize that Laban was a master schemer who would control his life for 20 years. Jacob failed to notice that Laban made no promise that he would give Rachel to Jacob at the end of the 7 years. He only agreed to give him Rachel for his wife. <u>The deceiver was deceived.</u> We see character in Jacob as he patiently served Laban for seven years. Jacob's love for Rachel took the burden out of the work and the time went quickly. <u>Marriage in the Lord is one of the most wonderful things in the world.</u> True marriages are made in heaven; few people today would be willing to do what Jacob did. <u>True love.</u>

Verse 21-30

The man who deceived his father was deceived by his father-in-law, and the man who passed himself off as the firstborn son now receives Laban's firstborn daughter to be his wife. <u>It's an escapable law of life that we eventually reap what we sow.</u> <u>Galatians 6:7-8.</u> God in His Grace forgives our sin when we confess them, <u>I John 1:9,</u> but God in His government allows us to suffer the painful consequences of those sins. Jacob had met his match in Laban. It was the custom of that day that the marriage of the older daughter was first. In the <u>darkness of the desert night</u> and the bride <u>heavily veiled,</u> the <u>deception was easy.</u>

Laban got his oldest daughter married off and got the services of Jacob for 7 years to <u>secure</u> Rachel, and <u>7 years before</u> marrying her. Can you imagine waking up in the morning and discovering that you had married the wrong woman? Laban made a fool of Jacob and there was nothing he could do about it. Jacob protested the way Laban had treated him, but he accepted his lot and went to work for another seven years. <u>You see little by little, Jacob was learning to submit to God's loving hand of discipline and was growing in faith and character.</u> Jacob would endure many years of hardship and conflict because of his situation, in-laws, wives and their maids. Laban must have thought very highly of his scheming. But listen to <u>Proverbs 21:30.</u> Notice, what Jacob's son Joseph would say many years later in <u>Genesis 50:20.</u> We can believe today <u>Romans 8:28.</u>

Verse 31

No doubt Leah was neglected, Rachel being the wife of Jacob's choice. <u>God was concerned for Leah.</u> The word, <u>"hated"</u> here does not mean abuse, but simply <u>Jacob loved Rachel more than he loved Leah</u>, and gave more attention and affection to Rachel. <u>Deuteronomy 21:15-17, Matthew 6:24, Luke 14:26.</u> Well the Lord was watching, and working it out for the good. <u>For all these children would be the founder's of the 12 tribes of Israel.</u>

Verse 32-35

<u>Reuben</u> means <u>"see-a son."</u> God hath seen my affliction. Leah was certain that this baby would cause her husband to love her, she was wrong. <u>Simeon</u> – means - <u>"one who hears."</u> Suggests that Leah had been talking to God about her misery. <u>Levi</u> – means – <u>"attached."</u> Leah was still hoping that Jacob would love her for her sons she had borne him. <u>Judah</u> – means – <u>"praise."</u> Instead of complaining to the Lord, she was now praising the Lord for His blessings.

CHAPTER 30

Verse 1-6

We see jealousy, Rachel wanted what Leah had, and Leah wanted what Rachel had.

With total unreasonableness Rachel vents her anger on Jacob. Jacob looks at her in anger and says, "Am I God?"

Now we come to something familiar, verse 3, this leads to more unhappiness. Rachel begins to scheme (like Daddy), and she now plays God. Any children her slave girl would bare would be hers. Dan was born and then Rachel declares with false assurance in verse 6. Dan – means – Judge. This name indicates that Rachel considered him to be evidence that God had vindicated her, or had judged her worthy of this child. God did not approve of this then, and does not now. Abraham, Isaac and Jacob all had trouble because of their sin.

No greater calamity could befall a Hebrew wife than to be barren.

We see Rachel's impatience, unlike her Aunt Rebekah, Jacob's mother. Rebekah was barren for 20 years, and just trusted God in faith.

Verse 14

"Mandrakes," the fruit that is suppose to promote fruitfulness of the womb. Rachel desires this fruit and makes a compact with Leah.

Verse 22

There were lessons for Rachel to learn, and God had taught her some things, namely <u>dependence</u> and <u>patience.</u> She acknowledges God and reaches out by faith for more, verses 22-24.

God is never in a hurry, He wants to accomplish His will in your life. He will accomplish His will in obedient children.

Verse 25-26

It was time for Jacob to go home. He had earned the right to freedom. He had made his decisions and his convictions were stirred.

Verse 27

Laban had other ideas, Laban wasn't interested in Jacob's God; he was interested only in the blessing he received because of Jacob's God. Laban may give respect unto God, but with an <u>unbelieving heart.</u>

Verse 28

Laban thought all he had to do was raise Jacob's wages. But by now Jacob had learned that the devil is a poor pay master. Jacob was now well prepared for his father-in-law.

Verse 29-31

Jacob's faith and his business sense had made its

impact. He had good testimony, and God is working in his life.

Verse 32-34

Jacob is now ready to submit himself to <u>the providence of God.</u> Jacob did not want Laban to <u>"give"</u> him anything. He had learned that God would supply what he wanted him to have. And so Jacob made a proposition to Laban that would give <u>God the opportunity</u> to bless him materially. This plan would bring blessing to Jacob without taking anything belonging to Laban. Jacob's pay would be those animals yet unborn that would be less desirable to Laban because of their markings. This way it would become Jacob's. Jacob agreed that none of the <u>solid-color</u> animals would be taken, only those future animals that would be born <u>speckled</u> or <u>striped</u> or <u>spotted</u> or <u>abnormally colored</u> in some way, would become Jacob's wages. These were considered inferior. This arrangement was to Laban's advantage to be sure. This was an act of faith on Jacob's part.

Verse 35-36

Laban did not trust Jacob, and so he had his flock separated.

Verse 37-43

Jacob's actions in peeling white strips in rods from the trees listed, and then placing them in the cattle's watering troughs shows perhaps his belief in ideas of prenatal influence. Jacob was an expert cattleman; he had overseen Laban's flock for several years and was of old age himself, he was over 90 years old. It is possible that certain chemicals in the wood of these trees were capable of affecting the animals. He did this with the strong animals. I don't believe we should criticize Jacob, for Laban gave him the opportunity to set his own wages. He quickly became a very prosperous rancher, within about four or five years. This whole process of Jacob's with the rods perhaps could have been a faith help in his work. Like the anointing oil in James. In any case, Jacob's hard work and faith in God brought God's blessing.

Remember, He that is faithful in a little shall be entrusted with more. He that is faithful in that which is another mans shall be entrusted with something of his own. Jacob, who had been a just servant, became a rich master.

CHAPTER 31

Verse 1-3

By this time Laban and his sons were becoming greatly concerned. Jacob had kept his part of the bargain faithfully. Laban's sons could see their inheritance slipping away. Jacob heard what they were saying; he was in a tough place. But just on time comes the Lord. God is always on time. It was now time for Jacob to begin the establishment of the promised nation in the Promised Land. "Time serves God."

Verse 3

We find divine direction with a divine promise. Jacob received orders from heaven. It is our duty to set ourselves under God's guidance. We see that God uses circumstances and people (ungodly people) to get his children where He wants them, and to get them to do what He wants. God stirred up the nest. God used Laban and his sons to make things uncomfortable for Jacob.

Verse 4-9

In obedience Jacob prepared to depart. Knowing he would not be allowed by Laban to leave openly with his flocks and family, he would have to leave unannounced. Laban had deceived and treated Jacob badly. But no matter what Laban tried to do to him, God had <u>protected</u> and <u>prospered</u> Jacob. Sounds like Joseph, his son.

Verse 10-13

<u>Here in these verses we see God.</u> God knew all about the animals, and was in control of them, and He prospered Jacob. God also revealed in this dream that He was well aware of Laban's treatment of him (Jacob) and reminded him of Bethel. God had taken care of Jacob; He prospered him greatly over the past 20 years, <u>despite many obstacles.</u> He did as He promised.

Verse 13-28:20-22

God was with him. <u>The exchange of words between God and man is important.</u> The Word of God to man <u>promises,</u> and the word of man to God. <u>A vow.</u> These exchanges are important to God. He records them in His books.

Verse 14-16

We can see that Rachel and Leah resented their father. <u>Dowry,</u> Laban received 14 years free labor from Jacob and had no intention of doing anything right by his daughters. Laban had no concern for his family, and the daughters were well ready to go with their husband.

We see that these wives of Jacob were ready to stand with him. <u>This is right.</u>

Verse 17-21

Rachel before leaving unknown to Jacob had stolen her father's "images" – small idol figurines, household deities. Laban had become a idolater, Rachel is influenced by him. Though she trusted Jacob's God she was also reluctant to completely give up her previous superstitions. Her attitude was little different from that of many new Christians today. Knows the Lord but not yet willing to live a life of separation from the world.

Verse 21

From Haran to Mt. Gilead is about 300 miles, a day's journey for men traveling unencumbered was about 30 miles.. With Jacob's caravan they would make only about 15 or 20 miles a day.

Verse 22-24

Laban was busy with sheep shearing, word had not reached him that Jacob and his family had departed until after 3 days.

Laban had a dream; God spoke to him and gave him a warning not to do Jacob any harm. God made it plain that Jacob was under His protection. Laban did not know God personally, but knew enough about Him to know he had better do what He said. We see here that God is indeed absolutely in control, of good men and bad men. Psalms 47.

Verse 25-30

Laban was angry and frustrated because God had barred him from carrying out his intentions. <u>Laban was a hypocrite.</u> His expressions of love for his daughters and grand children are unreal and way to late. <u>"Love expressed so late isn't worth much."</u>

Verse 31-32

Jacob knew that Laban would not just let them go. Jacob was sure that his servants much less his own family would not have stolen from Laban. <u>Jacob did not believe Laban.</u>

Verse 33-35

Rachel was quite a clever girl; she is the daughter of her father. What a family. Rachel did not know the trouble she was bringing on her husband. <u>Deceit</u> is sin, and sin always hurts, if you do not believe this you are being deceived.

Verse 36-42

Again, Jacob did not know what Rachel had done, so when Laban came back from his search empty handed, all the pent-up emotion which had built up over the years was poured out onto Laban. Jacob could hardly restrain himself. All the years of resentment against Laban was now going to come out. <u>Jacob reminded Laban</u> of his deceit concerning Leah which cost him 14 years to have Rachel, of the six years for the cattle. Then he reminded him of the loss which he took care of concerning the <u>attack of wild animals</u> upon his flock. Not to forget the changing of his wages ten times. <u>Ten broken agreements.</u> Jacob has grown much in these past years. <u>He left home in deceit but he did right all those years with Laban.</u> Jacob concluded his speech to Laban with a testimony that God had been with him. Jacob's increasing prosperity had been due to the Lord's blessing, and God confirmed this by His rebuke to Laban. Now let's think about something, <u>Jacob reaped what he sowed, but God was still with him.</u>

Dear Christian, if you drive down the road and go head on into another car, you will crash. God will take you to heaven, but you are still going to crash.

Verse 43-47

Laban tried to divert attention from Jacob's embarrassing facts by changing the subject. Though he realized he was in the wrong, a self-seeking hypocrite cannot bring himself to repent. He must try however to shift the blame from himself.

Laban proposed a <u>formal covenant</u> between himself and Jacob. The pillar was called by Laban, "The Heap of Testimony," in <u>Aramaic</u> or <u>Chaldaic</u> language of his ancestors. Jacob called it "The heap of witness," in Hebrew.

Verse 48-53

Laban the hypocrite continues as if Jacob could not be trusted and demands certain restrictions, and Jacob must not come back to Haran. Laban realized that God would bless Jacob. In his arrogance he tries to run the show, when in reality he is finished.

Verse 54-55

Jacob, in thanksgiving for God's final deliverance from Laban, offered sacrifices that evening. Laban came back in the morning somewhat softened although he did not apologize to Jacob, he did kiss his children and grand children goodbye He went home and no further mention is made of him or his son's in scripture. And so Laban passed out of Jacob's life and out of God's book.

CHAPTER 32

Jacob's two great enemies and or opponents were <u>Laban</u> and <u>Esau</u>, one outside the Promised Land, one within. Typifying the believers struggle against the world (Laban) and the flesh (Esau).

Verse 1-2

Jacob saw some of the angel's of God. Humanly speaking, Jacob was almost helpless, and so Jacob had to depend on the Lord.

"<u>Mahanaim</u>" – "<u>Two hosts.</u>" Jacob was testifying that he was being guarded not only by his own small host, but also God's infinitely powerful host. <u>Psalms 34:7.</u> God never comes with less than our need.

Jacob was faithful, God opened his eyes, and he saw the angels. <u>II Kings</u> <u>6:16-17.</u> Though invisible God's angelic hosts are real and powerful. <u>II Thessalonians 1:7, Psalms103:20, Hebrews 1:14.</u>

Verse 1

"<u>And Jacob went on his way...</u>" he turned over a page in his life only to discover he had to face Esau. Jacob had to learn a lesson that <u>God does not condemn sin in the sinner and condone it in the saint.</u> Jacob had to face in full the long account he had with Esau.

God cannot bless us with spiritual blessings <u>until we face our trespasses</u> and put it right where it is in our power.

Is it not wonderful that God comes to Jacob with assurance that <u>He will see him through it all?</u>

Verse 3-8

Jacob was wise in that he made all the precautions that were open to him, knowing that he would call upon God and trust him.

Jacob instructed his servants to address Esau as <u>Lord.</u> Of course Jacob was wanting to find favor in his brother's eyes. He also wanted Esau to know he was not interested in claiming any of Esau's possessions, for he was well.

Esau had heard that Jacob was coming back, and he did not know what to expect, and so assembled an army of his own.

And so when Jacob heard this report, he naturally jumped to the conclusion that Esau still intended to kill him. Jacob temporarily forgot God's protection. But again we see Jacob's wisdom in being precautious.

Verse 9-12

We see Jacob praying here, when humanly speaking he was in almost hopeless circumstances. Jacob was confident that he had been following God's lead in returning to his home country. But above all we see Jacob's prayer was based on God's Word. In verses 9 thru 12, this is a prayer according to God's Word.

He was claiming the Abrahamic Covenant. In verses 10 and 11 we see Jacob recognizing God's Grace, he humbly claimed God's promise. Oh how wonderful prayer is when it is in harmony with God's Word.

Verse 13-20

Jacob desired to live at peace and to share God's blessing with his brother Esau. The gift was very large, over 500 animals. He instructed his servants to tell Esau that the animals were a gift from Jacob who was following along behind them. These gifts were an expression of good will and reconciliation. A battle would have resulted in suffering and death. "Lord help us to have a spirit of restoration" Galatians 6:1.

Verse 21-23

Though the Bible does not say so specifically, it appears that after Jacob had done all he could he decided to spend the rest of the night in prayer. Romans 8:26.

Verse 24-32

Oh how important it is to be alone with God. Being alone is necessary, "...there wrestled a man with him..." Jesus Christ was wrestling with Jacob. Listen, God meets man as Man, the God-Man the Lord Jesus Christ. Jesus wrestled with Jacob, not Jacob wrestling with Jesus. This true story is not a picture of prevailing prayer, but rather it shows us that God's love is so persistent that He will even cripple a man to get his heart.

The wrestling was an endeavor on God's part to break down Jacob's opposition, to bring him to an end of himself, to break him of self-trust.

Jacob had his mind on his meeting Esau, but Jacob must meet God before he meets Esau. The lesson to learn is that we must meet God in order to be prepared for any and all other meetings. We see in this story the great lengths that God went too for Jacob to learn this. We need to learn from Jacob's trouble to put God first.

Again it is not that Jacob wrestled with the Angel, but that the Angel wrestled with Jacob. Jacob spent most of his adult life wrestling people, Esau, Isaac, Laban and his wives, so God came to him as a wrestler. God comes to us where we are. God is so good, so merciful. A.W. Tozer said, "The Lord cannot fully bless a man until He has first conquered him." God wrestled with Jacob to bring him to an end of himself, to take from him all self-trust, all confidence in his own cleverness and resource.

God had been trying to get Jacob to trust Him

all these years. He met him at Bethel with visions and promises. And yet Jacob did not give in to the Lord, he was still full of self. God met him again during those years in Haran using disappointment and trouble, and opposition in all with little effect. And now comes the crowning attempt to break his self-confidence. What did God want? What did God finally get? Jacob's willing surrender.

Verse 27-28

"…no more Jacob…" no more deceiver. To many Jacobs, to many deceivers, we need Israel, prince with God, power with God.

A prince with God is someone who God has control of therefore A Prince with God has Power with God.

Verse 30

Peniel –meaning – "The face of God." Jacob was amazed that he was actually allowed to see and touch God, and that he had survived to tell about it.

Verse 31-32

The sunshine on his face, and the Sonshine in his heart. He limped the rest of his life, constantly being reminded of his experience with the living God. John Newton, "we need to be constantly reminded of our tendency toward the self-life."

"Thigh" – strong point. God must come to our

strong point, and show us our weakness, for when we are weak, then we are strong. <u>II Corinthians 12:10, Hebrews 11:34.</u> Jacob is now ready to meet Esau.

Chapter 33

Verse 1-2

As one final precaution, Jacob arranges his wives and children in order. First the handmaids and their children, then Leah and her children, then Rachel and Joseph last. <u>The order tells the order of his love.</u>

Verse 3-7

<u>Custom</u> of the day, bowing seven times, a token of respect and recognition of Esau. Esau could not restrain himself any longer, he ran to Jacob and hugged and kissed his brother. <u>He had no bitterness</u> in his heart toward Jacob. Jacob's family showed the proper respect to Esau.

Verse 8-11

Jacob offers a large gift to Esau. Esau had prospered and had enough and refused, but Jacob insisted, finally Esau accepted. <u>Jacob desired reconciliation with Esau</u> and wanted to be assured of it, therefore he wanted his gift to be accepted by his brother. Esau realized his brother's sincerity and accepted the token gift.

Verse 12-17

Esau offered to go with Jacob, but this was impractical for one thing, because Jacob's group would have to move slowly, to slowly for Esau's group. Another because Jacob knew he would have to separate from Esau as far as God's future plans were concerned. They were still of <u>different natures,</u> and would <u>live differently.</u>

Verse 18-20

Jacob finally arrives safely in Canaan. Shechem was a prominent city. Later years was near Samaria. He built an Altar. <u>El-elohe-Israel</u> – "God, the God of Israel." God had called Jacob – Israel, and now Jacob calls God the God of Israel.

CHAPTER 34

The land was occupied with the ungodly.

Verse 1-4

Living so close to an ungodly city soon brought trouble. There was a <u>low moral</u> environment, and a <u>polygamous home</u>. <u>Dinah</u> never should have been allowed to go out as she did. <u>Moral Decay</u> begins in the matters that pertain to the home, <u>sexual liberty</u>. It is up to parents to see that their children are in proper surroundings. We don't blame Dinah, but rather her parents.

Verse 5-17

No word of apology from Hamor, he merely suggested marriage.

<u>Deceitfully</u>, like father like sons. God is not mentioned, God is not consulted. Jacob is silent, Jacob is a fool.

These sons's of Jacob are getting deep into trouble, using <u>holy things</u> to carry out <u>murder</u>.

Verse 18-24

Levi and Simeon made a serious mistake in taking advantage of Jacob. They were right for wanting to stand for their sister's good name, <u>but</u> wrong in their murderous plan. God would judge these Canaanites. It is always best to trust and wait upon God.

Verse 25-29

The son's of Jacob become murderers. Jacob's home life is coming to bear upon him. These sad things are written for our learning.

Verse 30-31

Jacob's <u>lack of leadership </u>in his home has cost a great price, <u>family</u> and <u>testimony</u> gone, throughout the land.

The boys are unrepentant in what they have done.

CHAPTER 35

Genesis 34 is godless; Genesis 35 is full of God. In this chapter we see Jacob begin to really live for God. Genesis 34 describes the <u>Shechem life.</u> Chapter 35 describes the <u>Bethel life.</u> There is a contrast between an unbeliever's life and a believer's life, but also we see a contrast between a <u>half-hearted</u> and a <u>whole-hearted</u> believer's life. God is gracious to Jacob, God said, <u>"… Arise, go up to Beth-el, and dwell there…"</u> God wants to bring back His children to the <u>privilege of fellowship.</u> As we are in the house of God, He desire's for those who are away from Him to return.

Verse 1

In verse one we have an <u>urgent call</u>. God could not let His servant rest in disobedience. He must bring him back to the point and place of faithful obedience. The only way of <u>restoration is repentance and faith</u>.

In Shechem it was the atmosphere of worldliness. You cannot hear the voice of God in this atmosphere.

Jacobs's grief over the events that happened in Shechem led him to go to God in confession and prayer, <u>no doubt.</u> In any case thank God for <u>His Grace.</u> Bethel no doubt held for Jacob some wonderful memories. <u>Revelation 2:4-5.</u> This is really what we need.

If we are not careful to stay in the will of God, God may allow a tragedy to get us back to Bethel.

God uses <u>conscience</u> or <u>circumstances</u> to remind us of our duties.

Vows are sometimes made when in trouble, but then are soon forgotten.

God said build an <u>altar.</u>

It was time for Jacob to move away from Shechem and go up to Bethel.

Verse 2-4

Jacob no doubt taught his family about Jehovah <u>but</u> was negligent in his home. This family like so many Christians today try to worship God and at the same time hang on the world. Many today are like this ancient family filled with the world's goods. All this had to be put away. <u>Colossians3:1-4.</u>

Remember Rebekah took her father's gods in chapter 31:34.

We see how a person's sin can carry on thru to generations to come.

"...<u>be clean, and change your garments:</u>" An inward change will affect an outward change. For the Christian the result of <u>I John 1:9,</u> will have an effect that will be visible.

Verse 3

Let us arise from our repentance and build an altar. Remember, Repentance-Unsaved=Salvation. Repentance-Saved= Fellowship.

Verse 4

The Lord is waiting for full surrender.

Verse 5

God prohibited Israel's enemies to come after them.

Verse 6-7

Oh what Grace, God appeared <u>again</u>. Oh how God loves us. <u>Isaiah 41:8-10.</u> God is in our lives, in our circumstances. What Blessed assurance, what favor, like sunshine after rain.

Verse 10

God reminds Jacob of his high calling. The Lord has to remind us again and again of our high calling, of our high position. <u>Philippians 3:14, II Timothy 1:9, Romans 8:17.</u>

Verse 11

<u>God Almighty</u> – Hebrew – <u>El Shaddai.</u> God is our infinite source, strong enough to provide our every need. <u>God is all-sufficient.</u>

Verse 12

Again God promised Jacob that he and his seed

would be a great multitude, would possess the land. God has given us much. Oh how much incentive we should have today as we comprehend all that we are and have in Him.

Verse 13

He "went up" as on a heavenly ladder, like he did 30 years before.

Verse 14-15

Jacob erected another stone pillar in commemoration of his meeting with God. He anointed the stone with oil symbolic of consecration. Jacob reaffirmed this place called Bethel.

Verse 16-20

Joseph was 15 years old when Benjamin was born. Rachel gave birth to Jacob's twelfth and last son. Children are a heritage of great blessing from the Lord. It cost Rachel her life. Always honor your mother; she almost died giving you life. Benjamin means, "Son of the right hand." Oh how great a blessing it is to have children. This is a touching story. Rachel was buried nearby, on the way to Bethlehem.

Verse 21-26

This fearful sin of Reuben cost him his birthright. Genesis 49:3-4. At first every advantage seemed to be with Leah, who was deceitfully pushed on Jacob, but we see at the length Rachel's son's come to the light. The Bible says, "...the last shall be first, and the first last..." Leah produced two murderers and an incestuous fornicator. Rachel's son's became and produced three tribes of Israel. Lord help us to do what we do because we love Jesus let us not do anything in deceit."

Verse 27-19

Finally Jacob comes home, and at the age 180 years, Isaac dies. The Patriarchal leadership now falls upon Jacob. There are three graves in this chapter, a family servant, a beloved wife, and venerable father. Thank God for heaven. Heaven is a place of reunion. Oh how wonderful to be saved. II Corinthians 5:8, Philippians 1:23, Psalms 116:15.

CHAPTER 36

Verse 1- 43

By the time Isaac died, Jacob and Esau were 120 years old. Compare, <u>Genesis 25:26; 35:28.</u>

When Saul became King of Israel he had to fight against Edom. <u>I Samuel 14:47</u>

We see in this chapter the names of the sons and grandsons of Esau, who had risen to prominence in the land of Edom as <u>"Dukes."</u>

"...the generations of Esau..." why listed? It is important that there be a distinction between the descendants of Jacob and Esau.

We see the importance of family, and that God is concerned about every individual.

CHAPTER 37

We come to the fascinating story of Joseph.

Verse 1

Although Jacob had trusted God's promise that he would inherit the land, he continued to live as a foreigner in the land of Canaan.

He did not own the land and only small portions were purchased.

God blessed them materially with great possessions, and they believed the promise of God would be fulfilled in God's own time. Hebrews 11:9-13. As we look at the 11th chapter of Hebrews we find; verses 3-22 are a spiritual commentary on the book of Genesis. Verses 23-29 show the truths in the Book of Exodus. Verses 30-40 cover the rest of the Old Testament.

"By faith," look at 11:1, Faith described two fold.

1. Faith relates to the future. "...faith is the substance of things hoped for..."

2. Faith relates to the invisible, "...the evidence of things not seen..." Faith makes unseen things real.

Every instance of faith comes under one of these two headings. "Faith is the title deed of things hoped for," And so this described Hebrews 11:13.

"And Jacob dwelt in the land…" Jacob was at rest, his wanderings were over, he was where the Lord wanted him. "It is good to be where the Lord wants you."

Verse 2

There are four main characters of Genesis, Abraham, Isaac, Jacob and Joseph.

God gives more personal details of Joseph than any other Bible character. One fourth of Genesis is devoted to Joseph. In Joseph's life we see the Hand of God working time and time and time again to work His will. In Joseph we see a wonderful type of Christ.

Jacob had been very disappointed in his three oldest sons. Joseph brought disturbing news of his brother's disturbing behavior.

Verse 3

Joseph was the elder son of Rachel, Jacob's beloved wife. Joseph's moral standards and spiritual insights were clearly far superior to those of his brothers.

Why is Joseph talked about so much in the Book of Genesis? He is not in the Messianic line. Because look at his life throughout these pages of script and you will see some aspect of the person or work of Christ. The great goal of the Holy Spirit in the believer's life is to make him/her like Christ.

Romans 8:28-29, "...*to be* conformed to the image
of his Son..." To be <u>conformed</u> or patterned after.
<u>Image</u> in conduct, behavior and attitude, to do al-
ways those things pleasing in His sight. <u>I John 3:22,
Romans 13:14, II Corinthians 3:18.</u>

Joseph was a Shepherd, <u>"feeding the flock."</u> This
tells us that he was a Shepherd over the flock. Wonderful picture of the Great Shepherd, <u>Jesus Christ.</u>

The coat of many colors is a symbol of his authority and favored position. Joseph's abilities and his
moral standards were superior to those of the others.

Verse 4

Joseph's brothers hated him. They were jealous,
<u>Acts 7:9,</u> envy and jealousy <u>Proverbs 14:30.</u>

Envy is a hive from which other sins swarm. Joseph hated by his brothers is a picture of Christ hated by His people. <u>Matthew 27:18, John 1:11.</u> The
opposite of envy is contentment, <u>I Timothy 6:6.</u>
When we know the Lord and are content with <u>His
will</u> for us we are peaceful and blessed.

Verse 5-8

Some think that Joseph made a mistake in telling the dream to his brethren. These dreams were
from God. I am sure these brothers thought of these
dreams later in Egypt.

<u>They hated him.</u> <u>John 15:19.</u>

For his dreams and his words. Again his dreams

came from God, and his words were his testimony about them. To testify for God will arouse hatred from the world.

These dreams were of <u>divine origin.</u> We cannot see that God instructed Joseph to tell those dreams, or not.

Verse 9-11

The reference to the mother in verse 10 seems to be Leah, who had taken the place of Rachel.

Israel could not understand the saying like <u>Mary,</u> in <u>Luke 2:19, 51.</u>

This repetition of the dream implies certainty of its fulfillment. <u>Genesis 41:32.</u>

Verse 13-17

In view of what happened in Shechem, which was about 50 to 60 miles away. Jacob was concerned about his sons and the flocks, so he sends Joseph to see what was going on.

Joseph was completely trustworthy and dependable. We notice from verse 13, <u>"Here am I"</u> that Joseph was in complete <u>obedience</u> and <u>humility</u> to his father.

Jesus came to do His Father's will. He came to seek out His brethren. While Joseph is a type of Christ, he is <u>just a man</u>; he did not know what was about to happen to him. <u>Jesus knew all that would come to pass.</u>

Verse 18-22

They had hated Joseph for a long time. Man has hated God for along time. Romans 8:7. Man's hatred for Christ was shown when Cain killed Abel, in Ishmael's animosity against Isaac, in Esau's hatred for Jacob. Man's hatred for Christ is strange.

We all have lessons to learn, Joseph had lessons to learn, and all the twelve tribes of Israel had lessons to learn.

We may conclude that Joseph had lessons to learn about pride.

The other son's of Jacob had to learn of the consequences of sin.

Strange Reuben of all the brothers would seem to have cause to resent Joseph more.

Reuben intended to help Joseph escape back to his father.

Verse 23-28

We see such callousness and cruelty. "A child of God who is out of the will of God can be very callous." How could they sit down and say grace and eat while hearing the cries of their little brother. They were like those whom the prophet spoke of many ages afterward. Amos 6:1-6. We notice what these brothers said many years afterward in Genesis 42:21. Oh but we see such kindness in these brothers. They thought an opportunity of avoiding the sin of murder. They were such good brothers, they moved from murder in verse 20, to letting him die in a pit verse 24, to selling him as a slave in verse 28. We see envy now reach full fruitage. Envy and jealously can cause you and me to as children of God do awful things to God's children. These fellows sold their brother.

Verse 29-33

Reuben rent his cloths, he was experiencing great grief. He was the oldest and would be responsible to his father. They conjured up a convenient lie. They killed a kid of the goats and dipped the coat in it. When Jacob saw the bloody coat he immediately concluded that Joseph was dead.

I wonder if he would have looked at the coat carefully and see that it was not torn, what he would think.

Reuben would have delivered Joseph, verse 22, but in God's providences Reuben was gone when Joseph was sold into slavery. God's plan always works out. God was going to work out great miracles in Joseph's life.

What about Joseph's dreams? Jacob should have discerned that God's hand was upon Joseph. We need to base our faith upon the Word of God, and not by experience. Mark 4:35-40.

Verse 34-36

Jacob rent his cloths, he went into great mourning. He lost Rachael, and now he thought he lost his favorite son. You'll never regret doing right. The polygamous home, the murderer, rape and deceit now seems to be crashing in on Jacob's heart. Jacob mourned so long that his family became concerned.

This is the first mention of any daughter's besides Dinah.

The chapter ends by letting us know that Joseph reached Egypt and was sold to a high official named Potipher.

Before we move on to chapter 38, I want us to notice something. We find in Joseph's life two great divisions.

The first is found in Genesis chapter 37 and chapters 39-41:13, and is summed up in one word, Humiliation. The second is found in chapters 41:14-50, and is summed up in one word, Exaltation.

In the first we see Joseph being trained and fitted for the position; in the second we see him as a ruler and administrator. The one teaches that before honor is humility Proverbs 18:12, the other teaches, that he that humbleth himself shall be exalted. Luke 14:11.

CHAPTER 38

We see from this chapter that God's Grace is always in the lives of people. In this chapter we see the shame of Judah and his sons. Jesus came from the tribe of Judah, <u>Hebrews 7:14.</u> Divine grace is seen rising above a man's sin to bring about His purpose. <u>"Man never would have thought of such a genealogy."</u>

We see danger surrounding the chosen family in Canaan. Verse 1, <u>"And it came to pass at that time…"</u> in other words the events of chapter 38 we re going on at the time Joseph's sale into Egypt.

Judah associating himself with the people of Canaan brought forth wicked son's , some of which the Lord killed.

<u>The sin of Judah and Tamar is a horror story.</u>

Verse 1-5

Judah takes a heathen woman for his wife.

Verse 6-7

Judah got a heathen wife (Tamar) for his son. His son <u>Er</u> was wicked and God killed him.

Verse 8-10

Judah instructed <u>Onan</u> his next son to marry Tamar as was the custom of that day. Onan married her but disobeyed in perpetuating the family name and God killed him.

Judah's wife died and Tamar who was in her father's house heard that Judah was out in Timnath shearing his sheep. She played the harlot, with her face covered. Judah being the kind of fellow who would commit fornication as casually as any Canaanite would. Not knowing it was Tamar, he went unto her and she conceived twins, <u>Pharez</u> and <u>Zarah.</u>

Judah repented in verse 26. In this chapter again we see Divine Grace rising above man's sin to bring about His purpose. <u>Tamar listed in the genealogy of Christ.</u>

Chapter 39

The marvel of young Joseph is that as unjust things happened to him, instead of complaining, he put his power into <u>the work at hand</u>. We read in verse 2, <u>"And the LORD was with Joseph, and he was a prosperous man..."</u> And so as the story unfolds it reveals Joseph's character.

Prosperity is not due to <u>circumstances</u> but rather <u>character</u>. So even though Joseph was in bad circumstances the Bible says that "The Lord prospered him." <u>"If you will honor God, he will honor you."</u>

Loyalty to God may bring its testing but God's Grace will enable us to overcome.

Joseph was in the pit but eventually came to the place of being ruler, and was the channel of blessing and deliverer of his brethren.

Verse 1-6

Joseph's life brought praise to Jehovah from <u>Potiphar a heathen man</u>. <u>Matthew 5:16.</u> Pray, Lord may men see thee in me.

Verse 7-10

Listen there is no doubt first of all that this was <u>a temptation to Joseph.</u> It was wide open for Joseph and he could have given in and gotten away with it as far as Potiphar's household is concerned. He could not have gotten away with it as far as God is concerned. Proverbs 15:3. Joseph knew better, he knew that it would be sin against God. And furthermore, sin against God's first institution marriage, is indeed sin against God. This is a very wicked sin. It's effects are enormous, I Corinthians 6:18, Psalms 51:4.

Verse 11-15

This seems unwise on Joseph's part to go into the house, when none of the others were there. Perhaps it could not be helped.

This day the situation came to a climax. Potiphar's wife was determined to have Joseph. The devils determination is no match for a yielded Holy Spirit filled child of God.

Joseph won, Joseph realized the danger and by the Grace of God he fled. II Timothy 2:22, I Corinthians 6:18-20.

God helps His children when they try to battle the flesh. We must do our part. Job 31:6, Romans 13:11-14.

Potiphar's wife now knowing it to be impossible for her to have Joseph, turned from desire to rage. She called out to the others for them to see Joseph's coat in her hands. She was a slick deceiver. The lies and deceit came to her mind quickly and she had a scheme.

Verse 16-20

Potiphar did not really believe his wife's story for if he had, he would have had Joseph killed. He merely put him into prison for appearance sake. No doubt he planned to pull him out of prison one day and have him work for him again. Joseph was very valuable to Potiphar. It is interesting Potiphar did not want Joseph to be killed, same as Pilate did not want Jesus to be killed, but for appearance sake Pilate gave in and Jesus was crucified.

We see from all this, the Providence of God, in the affairs of men. Proverbs 21:1. Joseph is a type of Christ but that is as far as it goes. There is nobody like Christ. Isaac as a type didn't die, Joseph didn't die, but Jesus did.

Verse 21-23

God allowed all of this to further develop Joseph in preparation of his great work ahead. Joseph submitted to the Lord and in difficult circumstances God blessed him. The prison overseer could see the capable and reliable Joseph, and no doubt had heard how well he did in Potiphar's house. The presence of God was so important for Joseph, and all of this available to every child of God. Matthew 28:20, Mark 16:19-20. Let us keep our eyes fixed on the Risen Christ, and believe that he is ever working by our side and confirming our words. Hebrews 2: 4.

He started this with the Apostles and now does his work with us and His word.

Chapter 40

Verse 1-2

The chief butler and chief baker had done something to offend the King, perhaps both were accused of something and after three day's the baker was found guilty.

Butler – In charge of vineyards, cupbearer. Baker – In charge of food, safety.

The offenses of these two were planned with Joseph in mind. Let us ever be aware that God is working in our lives.

Verse 3

"…the captain of the guard…" Look at Genesis 39:1. This was a prison that Potiphar was over. Again Potiphar did not believe his wife's story, he was part of having Joseph put in charge of the jail.

Verse 4

God vindicates His own. Let us always leave our cause with Him. Do right and leave it with God. Psalms 37:6-7.

Anybody with lesser faith would have given up, but Joseph remained true to Jehovah. He did not give up in despair.

Verse 5-7

Here Joseph is in the dungeon himself consoling the sad butler and baker. <u>II Corinthians 1:4.</u> <u>F.B. Meyer,</u> "Keep your sorrows for your Lord and yourself, but learn from your own experiences how to comfort those who are in any sorrow by the comfort with which you yourself have been comforted of God."

Verse 8

Joseph gave God the glory and God used him. <u>Joseph did not doubt God.</u> He believed in the sovereign authority of God.

Verse 14-15

First time Joseph speaks of the injustices that had happened. He did not derail his brothers or anybody else; he just told what had happened.

Verse 18

Joseph told the truth to the baker even though it was uncomfortable to tell him he was going to perish. Joseph told the truth. <u>Jesus</u> always tells the truth. <u>God cannot lie.</u> <u>His Word is truth.</u> <u>Luke 13:2-5.</u>

Verse 20-23

<u>We have two transgressors and Joseph.</u> Jesus hung on the cross between two thieves. The butler forgot Joseph. Joseph said remember me. <u>Luke 23:42-43.</u> Joseph was a good type of Christ, but <u>all types need to be saved.</u> There is nobody like <u>Christ.</u>

If you say to Him Lord remember me, <u>He will.</u>

Man will fail, but not The God-Man. Oh how we forget God. <u>Psalms 106:7,13,21.</u>

CHAPTER 41

Verse 1-8

Waiting upon the Lord certainly can be hard. I have no doubt these two years were hard for Joseph.

Dreams come in pairs, Joseph had two, then two more from the butler and the baker, and then Pharaoh's two. The repetition and theme of these two dreams left an impression on Pharaoh.

The writings of Moses have much historical character, giving truthfulness to life. In other words these dreams of Pharaoh are Egyptian in character.

"...stood by the river." representing the Nile River, the cow was sacred to the Egyptians, and corn was prevalent in Egypt.

Pharaoh was enjoying the dream, showing the fat cows to him representing the prosperity of Egypt, when the thin cow's devoured the fat cows this was alarming to Pharaoh.

Verse 8

"And it came to pass in the morning that his spirit was troubled..."

Verse 9-13

As soon as it was morning Pharaoh sent for his magicians and wise men of Egypt to interpret his dreams. The Egyptian occultists were helpless. Satan has power and as limited as it is yet he turns many to himself. Oh if we could stand in awe of the <u>limitless power of God.</u> He is All-Powerful, He loves us yet so many times <u>we doubt Him.</u>

The butler remembered but all the time God's all powerful hand was on everything that concerned His child, <u>Joseph</u>, it all worked out according to plan. <u>In the will of God, we can speak with the calm of eternity.</u> Remember what we see here, <u>is the perfect timing of God.</u> Not a moment too soon, not a moment too late, but in the fullness of time. <u>Galatians 4:4.</u> God acted.

When we are <u>faithful</u> over the little, and are <u>used</u> of God in the little things, then God will allow the bigger. <u>Matthew 25:23.</u>

Joseph was <u>faithful</u>, used of God with the <u>butler's</u> and <u>baker's</u> dreams, now its time for the bigger. <u>Pharaoh's dreams.</u>

Verse 14

"...and they brought him hastily out of the dungeon..."

Never forget two things, 1. You never know what a day will bring. 2. When God does something, He does it fast. When it is His time, <u>all of a sudden changes come</u> and they come quickly. When Jesus comes it will be sudden and the changes will be as described in <u>I Corinthians 15:52.</u> Joseph remained <u>true to God</u> and <u>his day came.</u> <u>Hebrews 11:6.</u>

Verse 15

Again we see the impression that these dream's left upon Pharaoh and how important they were to him. (They should they were <u>from God</u>). What a picture we have here, Pharaoh the King in all of <u>his splendor</u>, and <u>pride</u>, and <u>power</u>, sitting on his throne looking at a <u>despised Hebrew.</u> Think of it, he was seeking help from a <u>Hebrew in jail</u>.

Verse 16

<u>Joseph loved God,</u> therefore <u>he served God</u>. When a child of God loves and serves God he/she is not ashamed of God. <u>Romans 1:16.</u>

Here is Joseph standing before a <u>god-Pharaoh</u> and he without hesitation talks of the <u>true and living God.</u> He had only one thought, <u>the glory of God.</u>

Notice in verse 16, <u>"It is not in me: God shall give..."</u> <u>Romans 7:18.</u> Oh how we need to humble ourselves and give all credit and glory to God for that is where it all belongs.

Verse 25-32

The fact that the dream occurred twice to Pharaoh was an assurance that <u>God would fulfill it.</u>

Joseph made it very plain to Pharaoh and all around who could hear that all of this was from God. God sent the dream, God gave the interpretation and God will bring it to pass. Once God thru Joseph gave the interpretation, it all seemed clear to

Pharaoh and all around, nobody questioned Joseph. It makes perfect sense to accept Christ and live the Christian life. God showed Pharaoh what He was about to do. Ultimately all this was for bringing Jacob and his son's down to Egypt. To make a great nation of them. <u>Psalms 105:17-25.</u> God makes an individual, a church, and a nation thru trials. Storms are good; they sweep away that which is dead and useless. So God made His people a great nation and He used the Egyptians to help in the long process. The hardships did not hurt Joseph.

Verse 32-36

Joseph did not have himself in mind; he just relayed what God told him. God thru Joseph gave Pharaoh a plan and a man.

Six traits stand out which are model's for all time.

1. Integrity
2. Conscientiousness
3. Diligence
4. Nobility
5. Courage
6. Humility

Integrity – <u>Moral solidness</u>, or <u>purity</u>, <u>honesty</u>.

Conscientiousness – A strict regard to the decision of conscience, <u>a sense of injustice.</u>

Diligence – To <u>love earnestly</u>, to choose, constant effort to accomplish.

Nobility – Contempt of everything that dishonors character.

Courage – The heart, bravery, quality of mind which enables men to encounter danger and difficulties with firmness.

Humility – A deep sense of one's own unworthiness in the sight of God.

Verse 37

Pharaoh and his men were amazed and impressed with Joseph, his wise counsel left them with no doubt who should be in command of this job.

Verse 38

Pharaoh recognized that Joseph was a man of unique spiritual attributes. Pharaoh did not understand the doctrine of the Holy Spirit, but he recognized Joseph's possession of Divine power. Acts 4:13, I Timothy 6:12.

Here is a first mention-first mention of the Holy Spirits coming upon man.

Verse 39

With no hesitation Pharaoh acknowledged that none other than Joseph was qualified.

Joseph knew where it all came from, and now Pharaoh knew. "...God hath shewed thee all this..."

Verse 40-41

Pharaoh appointed Joseph over his entire king-dom, second only in authority to himself. This is truly amazing, an <u>unknown alien prisoner</u> sud-denly elevated over the entire land of Egypt. <u>If your known by God nothing else matters.</u> The best thing that happened to me today is that I have been with Jesus.

We again see the necessity for Joseph's years of <u>suffering</u> and <u>humiliation, learning patience.</u> Joseph was a humble man, tempered and mellowed. <u>He knew that God had prepared him.</u> Again Joseph's faithfulness pays off. If you are faithful and will re-main faithful, <u>God will reward you</u> and bless you beyond anything you can think. <u>I Corinthians 2:9, Isaiah 64:4.</u> Happiness of walking, communing with God.

Joseph knew God like he never had before, <u>he knew he could trust him.</u> He knew this because of all the years of testing, <u>he come to know God</u>, just as Job had come to know God.

Verse 42

<u>Signet ring</u> –Power to sign and seal official doc-uments. Vestures of fine linen, finest material in Egypt, a token of position. <u>Gold chain</u> – emblem of authority.

Verse 43

Pharaoh was showing the people that Joseph was now second in command. The bowing of the knee. Philippians 2:9-10.

Verse 44

Pharaoh made it clear that he was still the ruler, first in the kingdom, but also that people were to obey Joseph.

Verse 45

Joseph's Egyptian name means – "The supporter of life" or "The Saviour of the world."

The new name, the Egyptian wife all would help Joseph to be accepted by the people.

The type of this marriage is wonderful, here the bride taken from the people and elevated to share in a high and lofty position. A wonderful picture of the church.

"...Joseph went out over *all* the land of Egypt." Joseph got busy; he went out to see the resources.

Verse 46

In 13 years Joseph went from a Shepherd boy to being Prime Minister of Egypt. God highly exalted him. Jesus went from the cross to the throne. Acts 5:31.

Again, Joseph went out, a more detailed survey to make his plans.

Verse 47-49

God's plan always works, and is always the best. "Take up the fifth part of the land..." This plan worked wonderfully, notice verse 49; "...Joseph gathered corn as the sand of the sea..." He took up 20% over seven years and what results, "...as the sand of the sea..." God's math works the best.

Verse 50-52

These two son's of Joseph were destined to give their names to two of the most prominent tribes of Israel. Manasseh – "forgetting." Not that Joseph forgot what happened in Egypt but the bitterness was gone. Genesis 50:20. Ephraim – "double fruitfulness." He was fruitful in the land of my affliction. In Egypt Joseph had found "land of affliction," not of joy. His heart was ever in the land that God had promised to his father's and son's (descendants).

God wants us to be fruitful, in this life.

Verse 53-57

The years of plenty came to an end just as Joseph said. The people had grown accustomed to having all they needed. The famine came, this story warns us that the blessing of prosperity comes from the Lord and can be removed by the Lord, as He wills. It should teach us the value of saving a portion of what comes to our hands. Luke 16:11.

If Joseph had not prepared against the day of adversity then a lot of people would have starved. The famine came on all nations, but none of them made provisions for it. Of course God's plan was working and Jacob came from Canaan to Egypt.

It is something that 20% of the produce during the seven years of plenty met all the needs of the seven years of famine. Egypt's 20% for 7 years. This testifies to God's abundant provision in Egypt.

We also see that we can get by on less than we think.

Verse 55

As Pharaoh told the people to go to Joseph (type of Christ), God tells people to go to Jesus. Listen to John 6:35. In Christ all fullness is stored up. All the world come to Him. Isaiah 55:1.

Chapter 42

Verse 1-5

We now turn our attention from Egypt to Canaan. Jacob and his family as well as all in Canaan became aware that there was grain in Egypt, It became obvious that Jacob would have to send his son's to Egypt. They were reluctant to go, because their consciences were bothered. Christian, "Time does not take away a wrong that has not been set right." The road to Egypt would serve to stir up these brother's of Joseph, stir up their memories of how they did wrong to Joseph.

Oh we see here Providence, we see the Sovereignty of God unfold. God uses circumstances to steer whoever, and whatever, it takes to do His will. It is so good to be reminded of how Great and Powerful our Heavenly Father is.

We notice in verse 4 that Jacob was not about to take a chance sending Benjamin with all those brothers.

Verse 6

Little did these brothers know that they were fulfilling Joseph's dreams of more than 20 years ago.

Verse 7-9

The last time Joseph's brothers had seen their young brother was 17 years old; now Joseph is 37 years old. Joseph not knowing how they felt about him, not knowing their heart, did not immediately make himself known.

No doubt Joseph had anticipated their arrival in Egypt and no doubt being led of God, he desired reconciliation rather then vengeance. It was necessary that these brothers's of his be <u>tested as to their character.</u>

Verse 10-13

In these verses we see that the ten brothers thought Joseph was dead. The fact that they mention <u>twelve </u>brothers of their father, speaks of their truthfulness. Perhaps as the years rolled on these brothers have grown in character.

Verse 14-17

You cannot blame Joseph for not believing their story. As they had Joseph thrown into the <u>pit</u>, they are now thrown into prison. They ignored Joseph's pleas many years before, now their pleas of innocence are ignored. Their sin of the past was now brought before them powerfully. The Lord desires <u>justice and judgment</u> from His children. <u>Proverbs 21:3.</u> Of course as we will see, <u>Joseph loved his brothers</u>. Jesus loves His own, and knows what to do to teach us what <u>we need</u>. The key word of this chapter is in verse 15, "<u>proved.</u>"

Verse 18-22

By this time these ten brothers had been run through the ringer. They well remembered their sin against Joseph. Although many sins are recorded in Genesis, this is the only time we see the guilty confessing their sins. It is interesting the one (Joseph) who had gone thru trials and tribulations over the years is the one who speaks of God. Genesis 39:9, 40:8, 41:16, 32, 51. The ten never spoke of God.

Verse 23

It is too bad when God's people fail to remember that the Lord Jesus understands them completely. Psalms 103:14, 10. How unreal it is to reject the security that is in Christ. James 4:8.

Verse 24

Joseph's heart was touched at his brother's confession. Jesus wept over Jerusalem. Hebrews 4:12-16.

"Simeon" was bound. Simeon was the ringleader in the murder of the Shechemites, chapter 34, Jacob on his dying bed said nothing good about Simeon. 49:5, Simeon was probably the one who had Joseph thrown into the pit. Numbers 32:23.

Verse 25

"… and thus did he unto them." Joseph never said one thing about what his brother's did to him, he was not <u>vindictive</u>, and he only did what was right. <u>He did everything for their own good.</u>

<u>Isaiah 53:7</u>, "...yet he opened not his mouth..."

Verse 27-28

They were <u>afraid</u> when they saw the <u>money</u>. They right away thought of this as <u>the judgment of God.</u> When Jacob heard about it and when he saw the money he to <u>was startled.</u> Verse 35, We see here a lapse in Jacob's faith. He said in verse 36, <u>"...all these things are against me."</u> Never forget, <u>Romans 8:28</u>. "God never does anything to us; always He is doing something <u>for us.</u>" Even in chastening, <u>Hebrews 12:10-11.</u>

Dealings in money always brings about <u>arousment</u>, when they saw the money in their bags of grain, they right away thought they would be accused of being <u>thieves. It is not natural to get something for nothing. Isaiah 55:1.</u> Many people will not embrace the <u>simple gospel story</u> because they think they have <u>to do something</u> for it. <u>They think they have to work for their salvation.</u> These brothers had remorse but not repentance. They acknowledged God's hand in all this, but were not brought low enough to pour out their hearts about Joseph. <u>They still had not told the truth about Joseph.</u>

Verse 38

Jacob was still not going to let go of Benjamin. If

we are not careful we too may do as Jacob and not allow the will of God to operate in our lives. Of course
it is not hard to feel sorry for Jacob, but we must always remember that God is absolutely in charge of
everything. That helps us because He is our <u>loving
Heavenly Father.</u> <u>Luke 11:13.</u>

CHAPTER 43

Verse 1-5

Oh how powerful God is, you and I cannot stand against His famine or flood. Happy is the Christian who will bend to His will. Psalms 147:15-20.

God is not in a hurry, His famine in time, did its work. Another trip to Egypt became necessary. Remember this was God's plan.

Judah respectively laid out the facts. Jacob was going to have to comply.

Christian you and I might as well comply to God's will. You and I cannot possibly stand against it.

Verse 6-9

We see further, simply that Israel was going to have to give in to Joseph's request.

Verse 10

In serving God there are two pitfalls, one running ahead of God and lingering behind.

Verse 11

Grain and what you can make from it is the staple of life. They had the sweet stuff, but as Spurgeon said, "Cake is good now and then but makes poor daily food." Christ is the Bread of Life. John 6, Bread of life chapter. You need Christ to have eternal life.

Jacob in <u>verse 11</u> thought he would sweeten up the <u>Prime Minister.</u> Notice these goodies in verse 11 were exports of Canaan, 37:25.

Verse 12-14

So Jacob finally gives up Benjamin. Now we will see God work miracles for Jacob. When you and I as Christians let go of everything and let God have it all, you and I also will see miracles. <u>Prayer,</u> "Lord help me to let go, and trust you."

Note on chapter 42 – Chapter 42:8, Jesus is unknown by the Jew's, but the Tribulation will bring them around to the feet of Him whom they crucified. The famine brought Israel to Joseph.

Verse 15-17

We have here an <u>undeserved feast.</u> Oh how like the Gospel. <u>"All of Grace."</u>

It is interesting; this story occupies more space than any other in the Book of <u>Genesis.</u>

Verse 18

These men were afraid. It was not the <u>fear of the Lord.</u> <u>Proverbs 9:10.</u> Their fear was like a terror<u>.</u> <u>Some men must be shaken over the pit before coming to their senses.</u>

They were afraid as they were taken into Joseph's house. We can understand the strangeness of it all. They were farmers, men of the wild, now they step into absolute luxury, of unbounded wealth.

Verse 19-25

They thought it was all a trick, they thought that they would be made slaves. We find words of comfort in verse 23, from Joseph's stewards as they explained to him about the money. It sounds like Joseph's steward knew about God. No doubt Joseph talked about his God, and was a faithful witness. Oh how good God is to all people. He takes care of our every need. Physical and spiritual.

Verse 26-34

Once again Joseph's dreams were fulfilled, as he saw his brothers bowing down before him.

Joseph was emotionally stirred as he sat down to eat. We notice all the tradition and social order as all sat to eat.

Joseph was overjoyed to hear of his father doing well, and then he looked at his brother whom he had not seen in over 20 years, he could not take it. He left the room to weep.

God is good to all men, but especially to His own. Benjamin was Joseph's blood brother. You and me as Blood bought children are highly privileged.

CHAPTER 44

Verse 1

Joseph sends his brothers away with further Kindness and more trials as well. <u>All for a purpose</u>. Joseph could have done whatever he wanted to his brothers to punish them, but he tests them to bring them to repentance. <u>II Peter 3:9.</u>

Verse 2-3

We see further Joseph setting things up. Benjamin had his corn money in his sack and also a fine silver cup; it would look as if he had stolen it. Joseph's very own cup.

Verse 4-6

Joseph brings an accusation upon his brothers. All of this was preparing them for the coming <u>reconciliation</u>.

Verse 7-10

The brother's deny the accusation. We see the confidence of their being innocent in verse 9.

Verse 11-13

"<u>...they rent their clothes...</u>" This shows extreme distress. <u>Numbers 32:23.</u> Again all this is preparation from God. Oh how merciful and gracious our Heavenly Father is.

Trouble, that's how you define sin.

Verse 14

We see again the fulfillment of Joseph's dream in chapter 37.

Verse 15-16

Joseph comes to his brothers with a charge and a question. How do you think you can get away with crime? They of course still not knowing who Joseph was they thought he was an Egyptian. Joseph was saying he had the ability of divination. They were scared to death of this man Joseph.

Judah the spokesman for the brothers, felt helpless, there was no way they could prove their innocence. He confessed they deserved punishment. Even though they were innocent in this particular situation, they were guilty sinners and <u>"…God hath found out the iniquity…"</u> of them all! They felt the guilt of selling Joseph into slavery 20 plus years before, and now they thought they themselves would become slaves in Egypt.

Verse 17

Joseph tests them further, and offered again to let them go, <u>except Benjamin.</u>

Verse 18

We now read moving words of a father's love, as the love of Jacob for Joseph and Benjamin is recounted.

Verse 19-31

They would rather <u>not go back home</u>, than to go without Benjamin. They could not take the bitter grief it would cause their father. Judah was pleading for the life of Benjamin and his father. Joseph can see the hearts of his brothers, he can see what they told his father so many years ago, as to what happened to Joseph.

Verse 32-34

Judah now comes to the climax of his plea. We see here <u>substitution.</u> Judah wanted to claim the bag that had the <u>cup, as his own</u> instead of Benjamin. What a picture of the substitutionary death of the Lord Jesus Christ. I think of what Paul said in <u>Philemon 18.</u> Judah was becoming a man his father could be proud of. He was willing to follow through, bearing the blame forever if Benjamin could only return to his father. Again, what a beautiful picture of our Lovely Lord. <u>I John 3:16.</u> Joseph could no longer doubt that his brothers were changed men. He had subjected them to severe tests, and they passed the test.

Judah became the most Christ like of all the brothers. Of course Christ came from the tribe of Judah, and was called the Lion of the Tribe of Judah.

CHAPTER 45

This moving story is unparalleled in any kind of literature.

Verse 1-3

Highly emotional time, it was family time. Joseph had all his servants leave the room. Joseph was loud in his crying out after his family, the Egyptian servants could hear Joseph's cries and they went and told Pharaoh's house.

This is an indescribable scene, a most dramatic reunion. This event established the nation of Israel, of whom would come the Saviour one day.

We talked before as to the reason God brought Israel down to Egypt. He brought them to Egypt to strengthen and establish this nation.

They became strong through adversity, but also if they had not come down to Egypt they would have ended up scattering and merging with other people. God brought them together and kept them together and worked out His plan.

"…doth my father yet live?…" Joseph had heard general things of his father, but now he reveals himself and as a loving son he wants to learn of the details of his father. It is family time. Family time is important, make use of it.

They were "…troubled at his presence." They

were frightened and terrified as Joseph speaks to them. This dramatic confrontation pictures the coming day when Christ will reveal Himself to His people. Zechariah 12:10.

Verse 5-8

Joseph tries to ease his brothers, letting them know that he is not resentful against them. Joseph had learned that God allowed all of this to happen to him for a reason. All of it was planned by God. Joseph also wanted his brothers to understand that God was working on their behalf.

"A great deliverance…" Hebrews 2; 3, II Corinthians 1:10, Psalms 77:13.

"I am Joseph your brother…" in verse 4. In verse 3, "…they were troubled at his presence." Even though we are weak and sinful, and our Saviour is perfect, holy and God himself let us notice. Matthew 12:50, John 15:14-15.

Verse 9-15

Joseph gives instructions to his brothers. He gives them all that he felt his father needed to hear to get him and all the family to move to Egypt.

What tears of joy? You can only imagine what this was like for Benjamin who was very small when Joseph left. What a day for them all to remember. Think of Joseph, a type of Christ, he forgave all his brethren. His brothers did him wrong, really wrong, and he forgave them. Many people will not forgive somebody for far less injury. Ephesians 4:32.

Verse 16-24

News travels fast, Pharaoh highly esteemed Joseph. Joseph delivered the Egyptian nation, Pharaoh and all the people were grateful. Pharaoh was glad about Joseph's family and thought they would be a great addition to their nation. Pharaoh and his people wanted to show their appreciation to Joseph and bring his family too them and give them land and all they needed.

In verse 24 Joseph was telling his brothers not to doubt or fear, not to be troubled, his promises are sure. Oh how we can count on the Lord.

Verse 25-28

When Jacob heard the news his heart almost stopped.

Notice in verses 25 thru 27 he is called Jacob, but now in verse 28, Jacob is called Israel. In unbelief he was Jacob, when his spirit was revived, God once again called him Israel. Matthew 13:58.

CHAPTER 46

Verse 1-7

Israel was concerned about the will of God, and so he went out trusting in the Lord. When God through circumstances appears to be leading, <u>we can go with assurance.</u> Israel went out trusting that the Lord would shut the door if he were not to move. Israel stopped at the old <u>altar</u> at Beersheba on his journey. He offered <u>sacrifices</u> and <u>praise</u> and <u>thanksgiving.</u> Here is just where God appeared to him in a vision. (When you seek the Lord, you can always find Him). There at Beersheba God set Jacob's mind at ease about going down to Egypt. God promised that He would bring him back up out of Egypt when it was time. God assured Jacob that he would see Joseph again.

Verse 3

<u>Proverbs 3:5-6.</u> I am the Covenant God, He renews His Covenant. 212 years since <u>Genesis 12:2.</u>

Verse 8-25

We now have the listing of Jacob's family. These verses are important even though they might be boring to read. They are important because <u>family</u> is important. All people are important to God. The book of <u>Numbers</u> and the genealogy in <u>Matthew</u> and <u>Luke</u> are important for this reason.

We first see the children of <u>Leah</u>, Reuben – 4, Simeon – 6, Levi – 3, Judah – 5, Issachar – 4, Zebulum – 3. <u>Dinah</u>, Zilpah Leah's maid, Gad – 7, Asher – 4. <u>Rachel</u>, Joseph – 2, Benjamin – 10, Bilhah, Rachel's maid, Dan –1, Naphtali – 4.

Verse 26-27

These numbers do not include any of the wives of Jacob's sons and grandsons, nor the husbands of his daughter and granddaughters. Only those who were of <u>his seed</u> were listed.

Verse 28-30

As soon as Joseph heard his father was coming, he hitched up his chariot and went up to Goshen to meet him. When they met for the first time in over 22 years, the <u>joy was unspeakable.</u>

Verse 31-34

After this great meeting, there was business to attend too. Goshen was selected for the Jews, <u>good land.</u>

Shepherd's were an abomination to the Egyptians. Egypt pictures the world. The <u>Good</u> and <u>Great Shepherd, Jesus Christ</u> is an abomination to this world.

Christ His Word and every major doctrine therein is under attack in this world.

Chapter 47

Verse 1-6

Despite their differences, Pharaoh was very kind to Joseph's family.

Verse 7-10

What a meeting, the earth's greatest king and the man chosen by God to lead his people in that day. Each man could recognize the unusual position each held.

Jacob blessed Pharaoh. We see Jacob as quite the man of God, unashamedly representing God. Romans 1:16, II Corinthians 5:20.

Verse 11-12

We see here God's blessing upon His people, and we see the love between Joseph and his father and family. Oh how we ought to love our families and our church family and the family of God. I Timothy 5:8, I John 3:14.

Verse 13-21

The people had learned to trust Joseph. Joseph was a good business man and ran this operation well. Genesis 41:38, Romans 12:11.

It does every child of God well to learn this. It is well when each individual learns to pay their own way. Joseph made good gain for Pharaoh. You know the Lord Jesus is always blessing. "JESUS PAID IT ALL!"

Verse 22-26

The arrangements made were good for all. Pharaoh made profits, and the people did not starve to death, and were at the same time treated fairly, no one complained.

Verse 27-31

Jacob was about to die, and wisely began to make preparations. He called his son Joseph to his side and made him promise to take him and bury him in Canaan with his fathers.

The importance of this request is seen in verse 29. We remember Abraham in Genesis 24:2. Joseph took the solemn oath and assured Jacob that he would take him up out of Egypt and bury him in the Promised Land. Jacob wanted even his burial to be a testimony of his faith in God's promises.

CHAPTER 48

Verse 1-4

Joseph received word that his father was sick, and he dropped everything and rushed to his father's side. Joseph took his two sons' with him, Jacob made himself ready and when Joseph arrived he went right to the heart of things. He right away rehearses what God had done and promised to him. What a thrill it must have been for Jacob to see his favorite son coming with his son's. Jacob was a spiritual man, a man of faith. Oh how blessed it is to end up right. Jacob here pays special attention to God's promises. Notice, Paul gives tribute to Jacob's faith in <u>Hebrews 11:21.</u> By this act, Jacob shows faith in the promises of God to Abraham. This was faith and submission to the will of God.

Verse 5-7

These two grandsons' of Jacob would become a tribe each. Levi the priestly tribe was not counted as a tribe, and so you have the twelve tribes of Israel.

It was customary that the eldest son receive double portion of the inheritance, but as the case of Esau and Jacob the father could change this arrangement as he felt it should be. So Jacob was in his rights to transfer the birthrights of Reuben and Simeon to Joseph's sons. Since the fact that if Laban had not deceived Jacob, Joseph would have been the oldest son. And so it ends up that both Ephraim and Manasseh are counted as Jacob's sons.

Verse 8-12

Jacob was now very old and his eyes were dim, as he was told of Ephraim and Manasseh he hugged and kissed his grandsons. Oh what a happy occasion. Even though Joseph was a "big shot" he felt it necessary still to bow down before his father, and this pleased our Heavenly Father.

Verse 13-16

Rising Joseph guided Manasseh the oldest toward Jacob's right hand and Ephraim toward his left hand. Whether or not Jacob knew of the significance of it, God guided his hand to bless Ephraim as the eldest. Ephraim would become a leader over Manasseh. We see Christ mentioned in verse 16. The word "Redeemed" here first mention. Jesus has always been faithful. He calls upon his covenant keeping God.

Verse 17-20

Joseph thought it was a mistake, but it was God's will that it be this way. You can see that later.

Ephraim became the dominant tribe in the northern kingdom.

Verse 21-22

Jacob concludes by promising Joseph that God would be with him and bring him back to the land of his fathers. Jacob deeds a tract of land he conquered earlier to Joseph. John 4:5.

CHAPTER 49

Verse 1-2

Even though Jacob is speaking, he is speaking in the <u>Spirit.</u> What the brother's were about to hear left an impression upon them. Jacob was about to tell them what would happen to their seed, in the latter days.

Verse 3-4

<u>Reuben</u> was weak and unstable and lustful. Because he committed adultery and incest with his father's wife he forfeited the prerogatives of the birthright. In the history of Israel, the tribe of Reuben never produced a leader of any kind for the nation, no judge, prophet or prince is found. <u>Deuteronomy 27:20.</u>

Verse 5-7

Simeon and Levi, the two hot tempered brothers brought danger and shame upon their daddy and family, in their cruel <u>slaughter of the men of Shechem.</u> Israel disassociated himself from their actions. It would be for their good that they would be dispersed. Levi was the tribe chosen to be the priestly tribe.

In this we see the <u>marvelous grace of God.</u> It was the grace of God that could take a cruel person like Levi <u>and make him the head of the priestly tribe.</u> It is the grace of God that takes us sinners and saves us and makes us priests of God. I Peter 2:5.

Verse 8-12

Judah – "Praise." He would become the object of brother's praise. Not only would Judah's tribe be strong and courageous, but his land would be productive and faithful. Jesus came from the tribe of Judah. Revelation 5:5. Judah was always the dominant tribe.

Verse 13

Zebulun was to live by the sea and provide a haven for ships. The Jews have always been a blessing to this world not only spiritually but also practically.

Verse 14-15

Issachar would enjoy the good land assigned him but would not strive for it. He would eventually be pressed into servitude.

Verse 16-18

Dan a son of a concubine but was assured a place in the inheritance. The tribe of Dan produced a judge, Samson. Judges 18:30-31.

Verse 19

Gad – war like tribe, the Gadites were men of war. We shall have trouble child of God, but we shall prevail. Romans 8:37, I Chronicles 12:8, 14.

Verse 20

Asher, rich land, failed to take possession. We see deterioration because of ease.

Verse 21

Naphtali, Swiftness as warriors. Much of the Lord's ministry was in the land of Naphtali. Descendants, composers of eloquent speech and beautiful literature. "...he giveth godly words." Psalms 18:33.

Verse 22-26

Joseph, fruitfulness. Two tribes come from Joseph.

We also see here the description of Joseph and his triumph over the enmity of his brothers.

The history of these two tribes, Ephraim and Manasseh shows that many of Israel's leaders were from these tribes. Joshua, Deborah and Samuel came from Ephraim. Gideon from Manasseh.

"...whose branches run over the wall:" Prophetic of Christ, not only did he bear fruit within the vineyard Israel), but He also came over the wall to us Gentiles).

Verse 23

The struggles of Joseph are picturesque of the coming of Christ. Example, Joseph is innocent yet thrown in jail. Christ the innocent Lamb of God, and yet counted as the worse offender (middle cross).

Christ always did the will of His Father, and yet all man wanted to do was kill Him. Matthew 21:38.

Verse 24

"But his bow abode in strength..." Again what a testimony and a picture of Christ. Joseph in all his persecutions never said a hasty word. I Peter 2:23. Joseph went thru unbelievable difficulties and came out in glorious triumph. Jesus suffered the venom of man and his sin, and came through gloriously and triumphed at His Resurrection.

Verse 27

The tribe of Benjamin would be bold and strong, successful in warfare. Benjamin the last of them all and always ready to go. Psalms 68:24-27. Paul was of this tribe, Saul too.

Verse 28

Jacob concluded his blessings by calling his sons the "Twelve Tribes of Israel." The blessing comes in the warning of his son's and their children of bad traits. The children of Israel must have read these words of Jacob over the centuries.

Verse 29-33

Of course Jacob wanted to be buried with his family. But primarily we see an act of faith. It was to be a testimony to all the generations to come, that

Abraham, Isaac and Jacob had faith in God's promise that He would give the land to their seed.

CHAPTER 50

In <u>Genesis 50</u> we have the long account of <u>Ja-cob's burial.</u> The emphasis is <u>God's</u>. The emphasis is when a believer dies, the right thing to do is to treat the body with due honor. The testimony being that of the future resurrection of the body.

Verse 1-3

We see that even though Joseph was a believer and knew he would someday see his father again, he expressed his sorrow.

Death is the great enemy. Thank God it will die. <u>Revelation 21:4.</u>

We believers however sorrow not even as others which have no hope.

<u>I Thessalonians 4:13.</u>

It was customary in Egypt to embalm the dead. The Egyptians custom was to mourn for some 70 days. The Egyptians had come to respect Jacob.

Verse 4-6

Israel had become important to Egypt, and Jo-seph wanted to insure Pharaoh that they would all return. Pharaoh agreed heartily and sent people to the funeral to assure there was recognition of the honor Jacob had coming.

Verse 7-9

This was a great funeral procession of many miles.

Verse 10-11

Here at Abel-mizrain, "meadow of the Egyptians," they carried out a formal seven day period of mourning.

Verse 12-13

When Jacob's sons took Jacob and buried him in the Cave of Machpelah they were showing their love for their father and their faith in God's Promises covering the land which would someday go to their seed for an everlasting possession.

Verse 15-21

The brothers thought now that Jacob was dead Joseph would finally take vengeance upon them. Even though Joseph had been genuine in his forgiveness and treatment of his brothers, their sense of guilt was so strong that they could not believe Joseph had forgiven them.

Verse 20

Look at Jeremiah 29:11, it does not make any difference what event comes into the life of a believer. God means it for good. Romans 8:38-39.

THE BOOK OF BEGINNINGS

Verse 22-23

Abraham lived to be 175, Isaac 180, Jacob 147 and Joseph 110 years old. We see man's longevity declining. Joseph lived to see his great-grandchildren by both sons.

Verse 24-26

Joseph repeated the good promise of God, that someday the children of Israel would one day return to the land of Canaan. Joseph then asked his brothers to promise that they would bury him in Canaan.

BIBLIOGRAPHY

Barnhouse, Donald G. *Genesis A Devotional Exposition*. Zondervan Publishing House. 1975.

Crumley, G.F. The Pentateuch. *The Blessed Hope Foundation*. 1985.

DeHaan, M.R. *Portraits of Christ in Genesis*. Zondervan Publishing House. 1966.

Henderson, George. *Studies in Genesis*. B. McCall Barbour.

Henry, Matthew. *Matthew Henry's Commentary on the Whole Bible. Vol. 1.* Hendrickson Publishers. 1996.

Mackintosh, C.H. *Notes on the Pentateuch*. Loizeaux Brothers. 1989.

McGee, J. Vernon. *Thru the Bible With J. Vernon McGee Vol. 1.* Thru the Bible Radio. 1981.

Morris, Henry M. *The Genesis Record.* Baker Book House. 1981.